Fernando de Rojas
and the
Renaissance Vision

PENN STATE STUDIES
in ROMANCE LITERATURES

Editors

Frederick A. de Armas   Alan E. Knight

Refiguring the Hero:
From Peasant to Noble in
Lope de Vega and Calderón
by Dian Fox

Don Juan and the Point of Honor:
Seduction, Patriarchal Society,
and Literary Tradition
by James Mandrell

Narratives of Desire:
Nineteenth-Century Spanish
Fiction by Women
by Lou Charnon-Deutsch

Garcilaso de la Vega and the
Italian Renaissance
by Daniel L. Heiple

Allegories of Kingship:
Calderón and the
Anti-Machiavellian Tradition
by Stephen Rupp

Acts of Fiction:
Resistance and Resolution
from Sade to Baudelaire
by Scott Carpenter

Grotesque Purgatory:
A Study of Cervantes's *Don
Quixote*, Part II
by Henry W. Sullivan

Spanish Comedies and Historical
Contexts in the 1620s
by William R. Blue

The Cultural Politics of *Tel Quel:*
Literature and the Left in the
Wake of Engagement
by Danielle Marx-Scouras

Madrid 1900:
The Capital as Cradle of
Literature and Culture
by Michael Ugarte

Ideologies of History in the
Spanish Golden Age
by Anthony J. Cascardi

Medieval Spanish Epic:
Mythic Roots and Ritual Language
by Thomas Montgomery

Unfinished Revolutions:
Legacies of Upheaval in Modern
French Culture
*edited by Robert T. Denommé and
Roland H. Simon*

Stages of Desire:
The Mythological Tradition in
Classical and Contemporary
Spanish Theater
by Michael Kidd

Fictions of the Feminine in the
Nineteenth-Century Spanish Press
by Lou Charnon-Deutsch

The Novels and Plays of
Eduardo Manet:
An Adventure in Multiculturalism
by Phyllis Zatlin

The Poetics of Empire in the Indies:
Prophecy and Imitation in *La
Araucana* and *Os Lucíadas*
by James Nicolopulos

Ricardo Castells

Fernando de Rojas and the Renaissance Vision

Phantasm, Melancholy, and Didacticism in *Celestina*

The Pennsylvania State University Press
University Park, Pennsylvania

Publication of this book has been aided by a grant from the Program for
Cultural Cooperation between Spain's Ministry of Education and Culture
and United States Universities

Library of Congress Cataloging-in-Publication Data

Castells, Ricardo, 1954–
　　Fernando de Rojas and the Renaissance vision : phantasm, melancholy,
and didacticism in Celestina / Ricardo Castells.
　　　p.　　cm. — (Penn State studies in Romance literatures)
　　Includes bibliographical references (p.　) and index.
　　ISBN 0-271-01984-0 (cloth : alk. paper)
　　1. Rojas, Fernando de, d. 1541. Celestina.　2. European literature—
Renaissance, 1450–1600—History and criticism.　I. Title.　II. Series.
PQ6428 .C2894 2000
862'.2—dc21　　　　　　　　　　　　　　　　　　　　　　　　　　99-053721
　　　　　　　　　　　　　　　　　　　　　　　　　　　　　　　　　CIP

Copyright © 2000 The Pennsylvania State University
All rights reserved
Printed in the United States of America
Published by The Pennsylvania State University Press,
University Park, PA 16802-1003

It is the policy of The Pennsylvania State University Press to use acid-free
paper for the first printing of all clothbound books. Publications on uncoated
stock satisfy the minimum requirements of American National Standard for
Information Sciences—Permanence of Paper for Printed Library Materials,
ANSI Z39.48–1992.

Para mi familia

Contents

	Acknowledgments	ix
	Introduction	1
1	*La presencia angélica de aquella ymagen luziente:* *Celestina* and the Medieval Phantasmal Tradition	9
2	*De dónde son los fantasmas:* Dream Theory from Plato to the Renaissance	29
3	Calisto's Lovesickness and the Diagnosis of Heras and Crato, *Médicos*	47
4	Burton's *The Anatomy of Melancholy*: A Seventeenth-Century View of *Celestina*	63
5	Castiglione's *Il cortegiano* and the Depiction of Sensual Love in *Celestina*	79
6	*Echando mis sentidos por ventores y my juyzio a bolar:* Melancholy and Didacticism in *Celestina*	93
	Works Cited	115
	Index	123

Acknowledgments

Earlier versions of parts of this book have appeared in the following journals: "*E fu sì forte la errante fantasia: Celestina* and the Medieval Phantasmal Tradition," *Hispanófila* 118 (1996): 1–16; "Robert Burton's *The Anatomy of Melancholy:* A Seventeenth-Century View of *Celestina,*" *Celestinesca* 20 (1) (1996): 57–73; "*Il Cortegiano* de Castiglione y la representación del amor sensual en *La Celestina,*" *Castilla: Estudios de Literatura* 20 (1995): 33–45; and "El mal de amores de Calisto y el diagnóstico de Eras y Crato, médicos," *Hispania* 76 (1993): 55–60. I would like to thank the editors of the journals for permission to reprint this material in its final form. I would also like to thank Professor Frederick A. de Armas of The Pennsylvania State University for his very valuable comments on the original manuscript of this book.

Publication of this work was assisted by a grant from the Spanish Ministry of Culture. I would like to thank the Ministry for its support.

Introduction

Despite the extraordinary amount of critical attention that Fernando de Rojas's *Celestina* has received throughout this century, modern scholars have yet to resolve many of the work's apparent contradictions and inconsistencies. The resulting disagreement among literary critics has touched on a number of important topics, including the authorship of the *Comedia* and the *Tragicomedia*, the precise role of witchcraft in the text, the work's temporal development, and Calisto's possibly parodic nature. Because of the wide variety of critical opinion among literary scholars, Rojas's comments about the *Comedia*'s initial reception has become almost a commonplace for modern readers: "Y pues es antigua querella y visitada de largos tiempos, no quiero maravillarme si esta presente obra ha seýdo instrumento de lid o contienda a sus lectores para ponerlos en differencias, dando cada uno sentencia sobre ella a sabor de su voluntad. Unos dezían que era prolixa, otros breve, otros agradable, otros escura; de manera que cortarla a medida de tantas y tan differentes condiciones a solo Dios pertenesce" (80).[1]

Rojas's observations appear to be as true today as they were some five centuries ago. Perhaps the most convincing proof of this viewpoint is the fact that *Celestina*'s textual difficulties—and the resulting differences in critical opinion—are evident from the work's very first pages. Remarkably, *Celestina*'s opening scene has been the source of contradictory interpretations for almost fifty years, as Spanish Renaissance scholars have repeatedly attempted to find a logical temporal and spatial framework that would clarify the many difficulties in the work's opening conversation between Calisto and Melibea. The most commonly accepted interpretation of the first scene is provided

---

1. All references are to the Dorothy S. Severin edition in Cátedra. As is standard in modern scholarship, roman numerals refer to the act and arabic numerals to the page number.

by the printers' *argumento* to the first act, which indicates that Calisto enters the young woman's garden "empos dun falcon suyo, halló ý a Melibea, de cuyo amor preso, començóle de hablar; de la qual rigorosamente despedido, fue para su casa muy sangustiado" (I, 85).

While this modest *argumento* appears to present a plausible explanation for the brief but conflictive meeting between the two future lovers, some modern critics do not accept this reading of the opening scene. As Martín de Riquer (1957) has noted, Calisto and Melibea never refer to the *falcon* or *neblí* during their apparently chance encounter in the garden, as one would expect if the two protagonists had really met while Calisto was looking for a lost *ave de rapiña*. In fact, the short conversation in Act I does not even explain why Calisto would unexpectedly find himself alone in the garden with the young woman, nor does it mention the servants who presumably would accompany the *galán* while hawking. Moreover, Calisto's repeated allusions to his "secreto dolor" and to the "servicio, sacrificio, devoción y obras pías que por este lugar alcançar [tiene] a Dios offrecido" clearly indicate that the young man was already in love with Melibea before their encounter in *Celestina*'s first scene (I, 86). Since Calisto reveals that he hoped that the two of them would somehow meet, then Act I is obviously missing the complete prehistory of the young man's love for Melibea.

Given the conflicting and incomplete information contained in the opening conversation, it appears that the printers' simple description of the first scene does not fully agree with the more complex textual evidence found in the first act. Part of the explanation for the contradiction between the *argumento* and the primitive text may be that the printers' summary is not derived from the information contained in Act I, but rather from Pármeno's comments to Calisto in Act II: "Señor, porque perderse el otro día el neblí fue causa de tu entrada en la huerta de Melibea a le buscar; la entrada causa de la veer y hablar; la habla engendró amor; el amor parió tu pena" (II, 134–35). The printers' explanation for the first scene thus comes from Fernando de Rojas's continuation of *Celestina*, so these anomalies may be caused by a basic disagreement between the anonymous primitive text and Rojas's continuation of the work.

Faced with these contradictions and difficulties, some influential scholars and critics have provided original and often unique explanations for the textual problems in the work's opening conversation. Manuel Asensio (1952, 1953), for example, believes that Párneno's reference in Act II to a chance meeting between Calisto and Melibea "el otro día" (II, 134) means that the initial conversation represents a dramatic prologue separated in time and space from the rest of the work.

More recently, James R. Stamm (1988) presents a similar interpretation of the first scene. Stephen Gilman (1945, 1953, 1956), on the other hand, vigorously rejects Asensio's reading of Act I, and instead concludes—with noticeably little documentation or textual evidence—that *Celestina*'s first two scenes are linked by the work's subjective time frame. Gilman's view is shared with minor variations by María Rosa Lida de Malkiel (1962) and Dorothy Sherman Severin (1970).

While all of these scholars at least agree that Act I begins in Melibea's garden, Martín de Riquer (1957) finds reasons to reject the *argumento*'s standard explanation of the first scene. According to Riquer, the many religious allusions in Calisto's words to Melibea suggest a church as the scene's true location, an idea later accepted by A. A. Parker (1985).[2] Aristide Rumeau (1966) and Marcel Bataillon (1967) also reject the garden as the site of this key scene, with Rumeau concluding that the conversation may occur in or perhaps near a church. W. D. Truesdell (1973), on the other hand, does not accept either the garden or the church as a possible location. Opting for a dramatically different approach from those of all previous scholars, Truesdell writes that the undefined nature of the opening conversation suggests that the scene takes place on an abstract level "without spatial and/or temporal concretization" (265).

While it is unusual to have so many scholars disagree about something as apparently simple as when and where a literary work begins, there are several unique elements in *Celestina*'s first act that help to explain this ongoing controversy. In the first place, the opening conversation between Calisto and Melibea is the only scene in the entire work that does not provide its own specific temporal and spatial definition. Although *Celestina*'s authors normally use the characters' conversations to indicate clearly the time and place of each scene, the location of scene 1 is identified only by Calisto's ambiguous reference to a "tan conveniente lugar" (I, 86), a description that would apply equally well to a garden, a church, or virtually anywhere else in

---

2. I have indicated elsewhere (1993a) that Calisto's repeated religious allusions in the first scene represent a common expressions of love melancholy in contemporary European literature. This conventional use of sacred imagery would be inspired by the supposedly divine presence of the beloved, and not by the scene's location in or near a church. Giorgio Agamben also notes that religious allusions are particularly common among melancholics who experience the phantasmal presence of the beloved: "[M]elancholy appears essentially as an erotic process engaged in an ambiguous commerce with phantasms; and the double polarity, demonic-magic and angelic-contemplative, of the nature of the phantasm is responsible not only for the melancholics' morbid propensity for necromantic fascination but also for their aptitude for ecstatic illumination" (24).

Celestina's unnamed city. In addition, the conversation between Calisto and Melibea is so brief that there is no mention of exactly when it occurs, which means that the temporal separation between the first two scenes of Act I could be as short as a few minutes, or perhaps as long as a few days.

More important, as noted above, the entire first act—also known as the *antiguo auctor*'s primitive text or the *Auto*—comes from the anonymous *papeles* that Fernando de Rojas apparently found while he was a law student at the University of Salamanca. Since the original manuscript that Rojas copied is now lost, we do not know whether the *bachiller* altered the primitive text when he completed the first published versions of the *Comedia* and the *Tragicomedia de Calisto y Melibea*. Charles B. Faulhaber's recent discovery of the *Celestina* de Palacio manuscript (1990, 1991)—which according to Faulhaber may be Rojas's holograph copy of Act I, or perhaps a separate copy of the same primitive text that Rojas interpolated into the *Comedia* and the *Tragicomedia*—has yet to resolve this vital question.[3]

Miguel Garci-Gómez (1985, 1994) has attempted to resolve the numerous contradictions surrounding *Celestina*'s first scene by presenting the surprising yet logical conclusion that the opening conversation between the two future lovers represents Calisto's lovesick dream about his beloved Melibea. According to Garci-Gómez's reading of the initial scene, Calisto does not meet Melibea in her garden at the start of the work, because the *galán* never leaves his house during the entire first act. Instead, at the beginning of the *Auto*'s first morning, the *galán* sees the beatific vision of the young woman in his own bedroom—which would clearly be the most *conveniente lugar* for the lovesick young man to view the image of his beloved Melibea—before he awakens and calls out to his servant Sempronio at the beginning of the second scene.

I have accepted Garci-Gómez's reading of Act I in previous publications (1990, 1995), and I also indicate that Calisto's opening dream serves as the model for later Celestinesque works that begin with similar dreamlike episodes. There are comparable dream sequences in the anonymous *Comedia Thebaida*, *Comedia Serafina*, and *Comedia Ypólita* (published together in 1520 or 1521); Feliciano de Silva's *Segunda Celestina* (1534); Gaspar Gómez de Toledo's *Tercera Celestina* (1536); Sebastián Fernández's *Tragedia Policiana* (1547); Alonso de

---

3. See Alan Deyermond's discussion of the *Celestina* de Palacio (1991, 20–21), as well as the studies by Michael, McGrady, and García. See also Chapter 3 of the present study for additional analysis of this manuscript.

Villegas Selvago's *Comedia Selvagia* (1554); and Lope de Vega's *La Dorotea* (1632). While the protagonist's lovesick dream of his *amada* is repeated throughout the Celestinesque genre for more than a century, Rojas likewise includes comparable episodes in his own continuation of *Celestina*. Calisto experiences similar, early-morning dreams in Acts VII and VIII of *Celestina*, which suggests that Rojas also concludes that the primitive work begins with the *galán*'s lovesick dream about Melibea.

A central part of this new reading of *Celestina*'s opening scene is the idea that there is no temporal or spatial division between the *Auto*'s first two scenes, which means that this interpretation is not only a rejection of Asensio's belief that the first scene represents a dramatic prologue to the rest of the work, but also a challenge to Gilman's conclusion that *Celestina*'s subjective time frame joins the work's first two scenes. Nevertheless, if the opening conversation truly occurs in Calisto's troubled imagination, then this interpretation requires a definite connection between Calisto's lovelorn cry at the end of scene 1— "Yré como aquel contra quien solamente la adversa Fortuna pone su studio con odio cruel" (I, 87)—and his shout for Sempronio at the beginning of the second scene: "¡Sempronio, Sempronio, Sempronio! ¿Dónde está este maldicto?" (I, 87). Although there is no separation between these two scenes in the first edition of the *Comedia*, there appears to be no relation whatsoever between Calisto's sorrowful words to Melibea and his irate cry to Sempronio.

Despite this apparent contradiction, Rojas's continuation of *Celestina* presents the *galán* calling out to his servants the moment that he awakens from similar dreams in the second and third mornings of the *Comedia*. During the work's second morning, Pármeno returns to Calisto's house after spending the night with Areúsa. Sempronio tells the young man that their master is in his bedroom "devaneando entre sueños" (VIII, 218), but the master shouts for his servants as soon as he awakens from this fitful dream: "¿Quién habla en la sala? ¡Moços!" (VIII, 218). Calisto repeats the same pattern when, after speaking with Melibea outside her window the night before, he awakens on the third morning of the *Comedia*: "O dichoso y bienandante Calisto, si verdad es que no ha sido sueño lo passado. ¿Soñélo o no? ¿Fue fantaseado o passó en verdad? Pues no estuve solo; mis criados me [a]compañaron. . . . Quiero mandarlos llamar para más confirmar mi gozo. ¡Tristanico, moços, Tristanico, lavanta de aý!" (XIII, 276).

The Celestinesque genre also uses the master's shout for his servant as an indicator that the protagonist's lovesick dream sequence has ended. Although the pattern of the *galán*'s cry for his servants is repeated in the *Comedia Serafina*, the *Segunda Celestina*, the *Tercera Celestina*, and the *Tragedia Policiana*, perhaps the clearest example occurs in Alonso de Villegas Selvago's *Comedia Selvagia*. When the protagonist Selvago awakens the morning after meeting Isabela, he remarks: "¿Qué será esto? ¿Por ventura no estaba yo agora en el reino de mi señora, lleno de su gracia y gozando de su soberana gloria? Pues, ¿cómo me hallo en mi lecho? Sin duda que con algún fingido ensueño he sido engañado; bien será me certifique de segunda persona. ¡Mozos, mozos!" (134). Calisto's cry for Sempronio appears to have little connection with the preceding scene, but in reality this shout confirms that the young man has just stopped dreaming about his beloved Melibea.

In the present study, I follow a different but complementary approach to Rojas's work. Instead of analyzing the later Celestinesque genre, I begin by studying earlier fictional and nonfictional works that explain the behavior of *Celestina*'s lovesick protagonist. In Chapter 1, I indicate that the symptoms of lovesickness—particularly the *inamorato*'s dreams of his beloved—follow a medical and philosophical tradition that begins in classical Greece, is later appropriated by Arabic doctors and scholars, and then returns to Europe through the medieval Latin translations of Arabic medical texts. I cite numerous examples from a variety of fictional and nonfictional works, including the correspondence of Héloïse and Abélard, Chrétien de Troyes's *Cligés*, Dante's *La vita nuova*, Petrarca's *Rime in morte di Madonna Laura*, Boccaccio's *Fiammetta*, and Francisco López de Villalobos's gloss to his Spanish translation of *Anfitrión*. Thus in this chapter I link the literary and philosophical traditions of the Spanish Renaissance—which are often studied apart from the intellectual currents on the rest of the continent—with cultural and historical trends that shaped the development of European letters for centuries.

In Chapter 2, I explain why dreams were thought to be an exclusively visual phenomenon populated with phantasms and other visible images. The chapter begins with an analysis of Plato's and Aristotle's writings on dreams, then continues to early Christian writers and Arabic medical texts, and finishes with the principal medieval and Renaissance scholars in the field of dream theory. According to contemporary theories of dream formation and sense perception, Calisto's vision of Melibea appears to have both a physiological and spiritual basis. Sensual love creates a melancholic condition in the young man that leads him to see and hear Melibea's phantasm in his lovesick imagination. His rational soul, which in an ideal Neoplatonic order would lead him to a higher, spiritual love for God, is instead infected with the animal soul's insane passions. As a result of this sensual contamination, Calisto's intellect is incapable of steering him away from his destructive material desires, which leads to the *galán*'s tragic death outside of Melibea's walls.

In Chapter 3, I use the research from the first two chapters to resolve the confusion resulting from textual variations to Act I that appear in the first editions of the *Comedia* and the *Tragicomedia*. This discussion indicates that Heras and Crato—who are mentioned in the original edition of the *Comedia*, but who are later removed from subsequent printings—are two classical doctors of sight and hearing who would easily recognize Calisto's melancholic condition, for lovesickness was thought to be the result of the lover's visual and auditory contact with his beloved. The original reference to Heras and Crato in the first act of the *Comedia de Calisto y Melibea* was changed a number of times throughout the sixteenth century, because the book's editors probably did not realize that these characters were doctors of sight and hearing and therefore had a very logical reason for appearing in this passage.

I show in Chapter 4 how Robert Burton appropriates Rojas's work in his pioneering study on melancholy. Burton uses the Third Partition of *The Anatomy* to examine the symptoms, causes, and effects of heroical love, which is precisely the unusual and often confusing malady that affects Calisto. Since the *galán* remains a difficult and contradictory character for modern readers of *Celestina*, Burton's study may prove useful in the continuing critical effort to understand the enigmatic nature of the work's young protagonist. Significantly, Burton confirms that whether the *inamorato* is asleep or awake, he can "think and dream of nought else" but her (3:147), and as a result the young man always retains his beloved's likeness in his imagination.

In Chapter 5, I use Castiglione's *Il Cortegiano* to further explain Calisto's amorous melancholy. While modern scholars have never fully understood the *galán*'s contradictory conduct, Castiglione provides a description of Renaissance *inamorati* that helps to clarify Calisto's often enigmatic demeanor. Some modern scholars have judged Calisto to be an inept or parodic character, but this reading is based on a misunderstanding of the young man's melancholic condition. Castiglione writes that the madness of sensual love is a "calamità che ne' giovani meritano più compassione che biasimo" (339), an idea that should be remembered by the many scholars who have repeatedly belittled and ridiculed Calisto.

Despite the lack of logic and comprehension that Calisto exhibits during his periods of erotic melancholy, in Chapter 5 I demonstrate that his senseless death is particularly tragic because the *galán* must have been a noble and honorable young man before falling in love. He was certainly the "[d]iestro cavallero" that Pármeno mentions in the first act (I, 108), a characterization that is verified by Melibea's description of the terrible results of his death. It is obvious from her words in Act XX that Calisto was neither a fool nor an idiot, and much less an absurd or parodic character. Instead, he was a young aristocrat who exemplified the "gentileza," "cortesía," and "virtud" (XX, 333) that were expected of this powerful social class in Renaissance Europe.

The first five chapters of this volume contain analyses of *Celestina* as part of a European cultural and literary tradition that emphasizes the physiological basis of lovesickness and its accompanying dreams and visions. In the final chapter, I indicate that the work is also part of the related tradition of *reprobatio amoris*, which is the precise subject that Rojas describes in the "El autor a un su amigo" introductory letter as "las malas cogitaciones y vicios de amor" (75). I also suggest here that *Celestina*'s didactic quality confirms the thematic unity between Rojas's prologue and opening letter on the one hand, and Pleberio's lament in the final chapter on the other, two textual elements that scholars have never fully linked. The commonality of ideas in the prefatory material and the *planctus* creates a dramatic frame that encloses the action of the first fifteen acts of the *Comedia*, and later the first twenty acts of the *Tragicomedia*. This construct serves as a beginning and closing commentary on *Celestina* that not only emphasizes the text's instructional character, but also joins the work to a centuries-old tradition that condemns the catastrophic consequences of passionate love.

While modern critical commentators on Renaissance texts cannot hope to provide a faithful re-creation of contemporary approaches to literature, in this volume I attempt to place *Celestina* within its appropriate cultural and historical setting. The study reveals how the *Comedia* and the *Tragicomedia* relate to literary currents in the rest of Europe and provides a vision of a richer and clearer text that facilitates the work of the literary scholar as well as the general reader. In this monograph I thus attempt to present an innovative critical framework for future studies of *Celestina*, while respecting the cultural and intellectual traditions of the Spanish Renaissance.

1

La presencia angélica de aquella ymagen luziente

Celestina and the Medieval Phantasmal Tradition

As noted in the Introduction, the starting point for my analysis of Fernando de Rojas's *Celestina* is Miguel Garci-Gómez's idea that the work begins with an already enamored Calisto's dream or vision of Melibea. Although I demonstrate in the Introduction that the Celestinesque genre and Rojas's continuation of *Celestina* both provide extensive textual evidence to support Garci-Gómez's interpretation, there remains the vexing question of how the primitive text could lead this group of authors to an apparently common reading of the first scene. Although it seems unlikely that Rojas, for example, would repeat the *galán*'s lovesick dream in the *Comedia*'s second and third mornings unless he read a similar episode at the beginning of Act I, we still do not understand the specific textual elements in the opening scene that suggest that Calisto was in fact dreaming. Even if we disregard the interpretation provided by the printers' *argumento* to Act I—which of course would be missing from the anonymous manuscript copy of the *Auto*—there is apparently nothing in this scene that suggests to the modern reader that Calisto and Melibea's brief encounter occurs entirely in the young protagonist's feverish, early-morning imagination.

Nevertheless, despite the abstract and often confusing nature of the opening conversation, Garci-Gómez observes that the dream sequence has a possible model in the beginning of the *Paulus*, an anonymous humanistic comedy whose similarity with *Celestina* was previously noted by Menéndez Pelayo and Lida de Malkiel. According to Garci-Gómez's reading of the work, the *Auto*'s opening conversation represents a clear repetition of the first scene of this Latin comedy: "En ambas obras los jóvenes protagonistas se despiertan tras haber gozado de un sueño glorioso e increpan, en tono muy destemplado, a uno de los criados" (1985, 17 n. 5).

I have also examined (1991, 1995) the possible relationship between *Celestina*'s opening dream sequence and the *De Amore*, Andreas Capellanus's medieval love manual. According to Andreas, the feelings of love begin when a young man establishes direct visual contact with an attractive young woman. Her phantasm enters his body through the eyes and eventually captivates his thoughts to such an extent that this image becomes a constant mental presence in his wakeful imagination and in his nighttime dreams. The physiological and psychological presence of the woman's image in the lover's imagination would certainly explain the early-morning visions that appear in the *Paulus* and the *Auto*. Moreover, Andreas adds that a young man who suffers from the effects of erotic melancholy should seek the assistance of a helper and a go-between, so it appears that Calisto's relationship with Sempronio and Celestina follows the existing literature on lovesickness quite closely.

While both the *Paulus* and the *De Amore* represent possible model texts for the opening scene of *Celestina*, the repetition of lovesick dreams in two very different Latin works from France and Italy suggests that the oneiric sequence and the phantasmal presence of the beloved were typical manifestations of love melancholy in medieval European letters. If this interpretation is true, however, then this means that Calisto's opening dream is part of a longstanding literary and cultural tradition that Rojas and the later Celestinesque authors would easily recognize. To support this hypothesis, I will examine here a series of existing works that anticipate Calisto's opening dream, and I will show that the young lover's dream or vision of his beloved was a common element in European literature as far back as the classical period. I will also document the presence of earlier lovesick dreams with numerous examples taken from French and Italian prose and poetry of the twelfth and thirteenth centuries, as well as from Baroque studies on the literary and social phenomenon of lovesickness.

Two of the most comprehensive examinations of *amor hereos* or lovesickness in Renaissance and Baroque Europe are Robert Burton's

The Anatomy of Melancholy (first edition, 1621) and Jacques Ferrand's *De la Maladie D'Amour, ou Melancholie Erotique* (1623), which was published in English in 1640 as *Erotomania, or a Treatise Discoursing of the Essence, Causes, Symptomes, Prognosticks, and Cure of Love or Erotique Melancholy*.[1] The writers of both of these works study the origins of lovesickness and its manifestations in European letters from the classical period up to the sixteenth century, and both authors emphasize that the lover's dreams of his lady are a natural part of this ailment. According to Ferrand:

> The causes of those continuall wakings which oppresse Lovers, making them more Melancholy, sad, leane, and Dry ... are the diverse Imaginations and Fantasies that steale into the Braine, and never suffer them to take any quiet repose.... And if by chance they be surprised by any light slumber, which is the provision Nature hath made for the repairing of Animall spirits, which in them are wasted and much impaired, by the violence of their Imagination, and excessive wakings that slumber is attended on by a thousand Phantasmes, and fearefull dreames; so that they awake oftimes more discontented, sad, pensive, melancholy, and fearefull than before; and for the most part they find themselves more tormented sleeping than waking. (131–32)

Burton agrees that dreams are a normal part of love melancholy, and he indicates that the most frequent manifestation of this phenomenon occurs in the lover's dreams about his lady. Burton observes that lovesick young men, whether suffering from bouts of amorous melancholy or from brief moments of uncontrolled euphoria, typically experience the continual presence of the beloved in their imagination: "Howsoever his present state be pleasing or displeasing, 'tis continuate as long as he loves, he can do nothing, think of nothing but her" (III.2.3; 558). More important, Burton indicates that this continual contemplation of the beloved occurs not only in the young man's daytime imagination, but also in his nighttime dreams: "[D]esire hath no rest, she is his cynosure, hesperus and vesper, his morning and evening star, his goddess, his mistress, his life, his soul, his everything; dreaming, waking, she is always in his mouth" (III.2.3; 558).[2]

---

1. See Chapter 4 for an analysis of *Celestina*'s presence in Burton's *The Anatomy of Melancholy*.
2. Studies on lovesickness also existed in Renaissance Spain, including a 1495 translation of Bernardus Gordonius's classic study of *amor hereos* in his *Lilio de Medicina*. In

Burton provides numerous illustrations of the lover's dreamworld imagination that are taken from both classical and modern literature. In Achilles Tatius's *Clitophon and Leucippe*, for example, the protagonist Clitophon is immediately overcome by his first visual contact with the young woman's beauty: "Directly I saw her, I was lost; for beauty wounds deeper than any arrow and strikes down through the eyes into the soul; the eye is the passage for a lover's wound" (I.4; 15).[3] That evening, Clitophon cannot sleep, because Leucippe's image overwhelms the young man's anguished imagination, but when he finally falls asleep he dreams only of her: "Hardly about daybreak did sleep of a kind take pity upon me and give me a little respite: but not even then could I banish the maiden from my mind; Leucippe was all my dreams—I spoke with her, I sported with her, I ate with her, I touched her; yes, I obtained a greater degree of happiness than in the daytime, for I kissed her, and it was a real kiss: the natural result was that when my servant came to wake me, I upbraided him bitterly for his untimely coming, so thus I lost so sweet a dream" (I.6; 21).[4]

According to Burton's study, it is perfectly normal for a young man to speak with his beloved's phantasy in his dreams. A lover's melancholic fixation becomes so strong that the woman's image overwhelms his disturbed thoughts, and—as occurs to Clitophon with his beloved Leucippe—this illusory image appears to be absolutely real: "In the meantime he raves on her; her sweet face, eyes, actions, gestures, hands, feet, speech, length, breadth, height, depth, and the rest of her dimensions, are so surveyed, measured, and taken, by that Astrolabe

---

addition, Alfonso de Madrigal del Tostado (c. 1400–1455) anticipates the work of Ferrand and Burton by analyzing the causes and effects of love melancholy with numerous examples taken from classical letters. For the relationship between Tostado and *Celestina*, see Dorothy Severin's edition of Rojas's work (97 n. 36).

3. This sentiment is typical of classical theories of sense perception that were carried over to the Middle Ages and the Renaissance. For studies on medieval theories of love and lovesickness, see Lowes; Babb, chapter 4, "The Lover's Malady in Medical Theory," 128–42; Jackson, chapter 14, "Love-Melancholy," 352–72; and especially Mary Frances Wack's *Lovesickness in the Middle Ages*. See also Chapters 2 and 3 of the present study.

4. As can be seen, this dream sequence anticipates not only the opening of the *Paulus*, but also Calisto's reporting of his dreams about Melibea in *Celestina*. In the sixth act, Calisto surprises Celestina when he tells her that he has touched Melibea, but he then explains that the whole thing has occurred in his dreamworld imagination:

CELESTINA: ¿Que la has tocado, dizes? Mucho me espantas.
CALISTO: Entre sueños, digo.... En sueños la veo tantas noches que temo no me acontezca como a Alcibíades [o a Sócrates], que [el uno] soñó que se ve va embuelto en el manto de su amiga y otro día matáronle. (VI, 185–86)

of phantasy, and so violently sometimes, with such earnestness and eagerness, such continuance, so strong an imagination, that at length he thinks he sees her indeed; he talks with her, he embraceth her" (III.2.3; 559).

While the lover's dreamlike vision of his beloved is originally found in classical literature, this phantasmal tradition reappears in European letters in twelfth-century France. The clearest example of this phenomenon occurs in the correspondence of the nun Héloïse (1101–64) with the priest and theologian Abélard (1079–1142), her husband and the father of her child. Much like Calisto, Héloïse is continually haunted by her lover's phantasm, whose sensual image accompanies her even as she sleeps:

> Quant à moi, ces voluptés de l'amour que nous avons goûtées ensemble m'ont été si douces, que le souvenir ne peut m'en déplaire ni même s'effacer de ma mémoire. De quelque côté que je me tourne, elles se présentent, elles s'imposent à mes regards avec les désirs qu'elles réveillent; *leurs trompeuses images n'épargnent même pas mon sommeil.* . . . Ce n'est pas seulement ce que nous avons fait, ce son les heures, ce son les lieux témoins de ce que nous avons fait, *qui sont si profondément gravés dans mon coeur avec ton image,* que je me retrouve avec toi dans les mêmes lieux, aux mêmes heures, faisant les mêmes choses: *méme en dormant, je ne trouve point le repos.* Parfois les mouvements de mon corps trahissent les pensées de mon âme, des mots m'echappent que je n'ai pu retenir. (Abélard and Héloïse n.d., 80–81; emphasis added)

> (In my case, the pleasures of lovers which we shared have been too sweet—they can never displease me, and can scarcely be banished from my thoughts. Wherever I turn they are always there before my eyes, bringing with them awakened longings and *fantasies which will not even let me sleep.* . . . Everything we did and also the times and places are *stamped on my heart along with your image,* so that I live through it all again with you. *Even in sleep I know no respite.* Sometimes my thoughts are betrayed in a movement of my body, or they break out in an unguarded word. [1974, 133; emphasis added])

The writings of Héloïse and Andreas reveal that the dreams and visions of heroical love were an accepted psychological experience in the Middle Ages, which would explain why there is so little difference between these apparently factual accounts and the phantasmal images that appear in medieval French and Italian poetry. Both the *fin amor* and *dolce stil nuovo* lyrical traditions insist on the importance of the beloved's image in the lovesick poet's imagination, which means that this phantasmic vision often takes the place of the lady's material presence. In the words of Giorgio Agamben,

> It is not possible . . . to understand the amorous ceremonial that the troubadour lyric and the poets of the "dolce stil nuovo" left as a legacy to modern Western poetry unless notice is taken that since its origins this ceremonial presented itself as a phantasmatic process. Not an external body, but an internal image, that is, the phantasm impressed on the phantastic spirits by the gaze, is the origin and the object of falling in love; only the attentive elaboration and immoderate contemplation of this phantasmatic mental simulacrum were held capable of generating an authentic amorous passion. (23–24)

While Robert Pogue Harrison has noted that Agamben perhaps fails to consider the physical dimension that also exists in some Provençal and stilnovist poetry (53), the importance of these visions, dreams, and phantasms is undeniable. These lyrical illusions, which often appear while the poet is thinking about his or her beloved in bed or in his or her room, can be seen for example in the writings of an anonymous twelfth-century Provençal woman poet:

> The whole night long I sigh and dream
> and waken with a start
> Thinking my friend had roused me from my sleep
> O Heaven! how soon my malady would be cured.
> Should he come to me one night. Ah me!
> Into my curtained chamber he once stole
> Like unto a thief
> Into my chamber richly adorned . . .
> And hence, unable now to gaze at you admiringly
> I die of pain at my soul's aridity. (Sullerot 57)

There is another illustration of the importance of lovesick dreams in French poetry in Chrétien de Troyes's *Cligés*, a twelfth-century romance. At the beginning of the poem, Alixandre and Soredamors are sailing aboard the same ship, and the young woman quickly falls in love with the brave Greek knight. Alixandre also falls in love with

Soredamors during the voyage, but although the two young lovers trade longing glances and become pale with erotic melancholy, at first they do not realize that this attraction is mutual. Both attempt to hide their love when they are together during the day, but they are unable to suppress these feelings when they are alone in the evening: "Mes la nuit est la plainte granz, / Que chascuns fet a lui meïmes" (606–7) ("But at night suffering overflowed / Their hearts and filled their minds" [611–12]). At these times, Alixandre lies in bed and recalls Soredamor's lovely image in his nighttime imagination:

> D'Alixandre vos dirai primes
> Comant il se plaint et demante.
> Amors celi li represante
> Por cui se sant si fort grevé,
> Que de son cuer l'a eslevé,
> Ne nel lesse an lit reposer:
> Tant li delite a remanbrer
> La biauté et la contenance
> Celi, ou n'a point d'esperance
> Que ja biens l'an doie venir. (610–19)

> (Let me tell you, first, the unspoken
> Words he said to himself
> As Love conjured pictures
> Of her for whom he was suffering,
> So wounding his heart that even
> Lying in bed he could not
> Sleep, yet happily remembering
> That face, that beauty he never
> Expected could ever be his. [613–21])

There is another dream sequence in the anonymous thirteenth-century fabliau *De Guillaume au faucon*. Guillaume, a young squire who has been secretly in love with his lady for seven years, is cruelly rejected when he finally confesses his love to her. Stung by the force of her rejection, the squire decides to fast until he wins her love, but on the third day of his torment he experiences an imaginary vision of his lady:

> Guillaumes est en grant effroi
> Quant li hueil li tornent un poi;
> La dame, qui tant par est gente,

> Ce li est vis que il la sente
> Entre ses braz dedenz son lit,
> Et qui'il en fait tot son delit.
> Tant com ce dure est molt a ese,
> Quar it l'acole et si la baise;
> Et, quant cel avisïon faut,
> Donques soupire et si tressalt
> Estent ses braz, n'en treuve mie;
> Fols est qui chace la folie. (353–64)

> (William lay in bed and shook,
> And when he rolled his eyes to look,
> The lovely lady, full of charms—
> He thought he felt her in his arms,
> Lying there with him and granting
> Everything that he was wanting.
> And while this lasted, it was bliss
> To hold her, trading kiss for kiss.
> And when at last the vision waned,
> He trembled, sighed, reached out his hand,
> But air is all that he embraced.
> Foolishness is what fools chase! [351–62])

Although the phantasmal images of heroical love are a common topic in French romances, fabliaux, and Provençal poetry, the best-known example of this malady occurs in the life and work of Dante. The poet writes in *La vita nuova* that he fell in love with Beatrice at the age of nine "quando a li miei occhi apparve prima la gloriosa donna della mia mente" (46) ("when to my eyes first appeared the glorious lady of my mind" [47]). While Dante indicates that he falls in love through the visual contact with his lady, he describes Beatrice as *la gloriosa donna della mia mente* because he sees her in his imagination much more than he does in real life. The poet's heart and mind constantly endeavor to recapture the lovely image of Beatrice, but this usually occurs not through her direct physical presence, but rather through "la sua imagine, la quale continuamente meco stava" (48) ("her image, which continually stayed with me" [49]). These visions often take place in Dante's own chamber, where he experiences the "soave sonno" ("sweet dream") and the "maravigliosa visione" ("marvelous vision") of the spirit of Love, who comes out of a cloud to show the poet the sleeping figure of Beatrice (48 [49]). The spirit then awakens Beatrice so that the young woman will consume Dante's heart before she ascends into heaven, at which time Dante awakens from the dream: "[O]nde io sostenea sì grande angoscia, che lo mio deboletto sonno non poteo sostenere, anzi si ruppe e fui disvegliato" (50) ("I suffered so much anguish that I could not sustain my fragile sleep, which indeed broke and I awakened" [51]).

As Dante suffers because of his overpowering love for Beatrice, his room turns into a "camera de le lagrime" (72) ("room of tears" [73]), a place where he experiences the confusing dreams and visions of erotic melancholy. The poet eventually becomes physically sick—as often occurs to a young lover who suffers from the effects of *amor hereos*—and during his illness he observes in his "fantasia" a frightening scene of disheveled, weeping women in the middle of a horrible earthquake (98). During this terrible "fallace imaginare" (98) ("false imagining" [99]), Dante sees an old friend who tells him that Beatrice has died, and the poet then witnesses the young woman's recumbent body wrapped in a white veil:

> [M]i parea andare per vedere lo corpo ne lo quale era stata quella nobilissima e beata anima; e fu sì forte la erronea fantasia, che mi mostrò questa donna morta ... e pareami che la sua faccia avesse tanto aspetto d'umiltade, che parea che dicesse: "Io sono a vedere lo principio della pace." (96)

> (I seemed to go and see the body which had dwelled in that most noble and blessed soul; and so strong was the erroneous fantasy that it showed me that lady dead ... and it appeared that her face had so much the aspect of humility that she seemed to say: "I am beholding the font of peace." [97])

Dante is distraught when Beatrice tragically dies a short time later, just as he had anticipated in his horrible dream. Soon afterward, however, a younger woman catches his eye and begins to stir similar amorous passions in the poet. Despite the comfort that he receives from the young woman's compassionate gaze, however, Dante experiences another vision that reminds him that he must always maintain Beatrice's memory after her death just as he did during her lifetime:

> Contra questo avversario de la ragione si levoe un die, quasi ne l'ora di nona, una forte immagionazione in meo, che mi parve vedere questa gloriosa Beatrice con quelle vestimenta sanguigne co le quali apparve prima a li occhi miei; e pareami giovani in simile etade in quale io prima la vidi. (136)

(Against this adversary of reason arose in me one day, at about the ninth hour, a powerful imagining: that is, I seemed to see this glorious Beatrice with those crimson vestments in which she first appeared before my eyes; and to me she seemed young and of the same age as when I first saw her. [137])

As a result of this amorous vision, Dante writes that "si rivolsero tutti li miei pensamenti a la loro gentilissima Beatrice" (136) ("all my thoughts began to revert to their most gentle Beatrice" [137]), and he again begins to suffer the "sospiri" ("sighs") and the "pianto" ("weeping") typical of heroical love (139 [140]). The poet thus confirms his eternal love for Beatrice through his dreamworld imagination of her phantasmal image, and his eyes never again seek the beauty of other women.

Dante's visions of Beatrice after her death are echoed in Petrarca's *Rime in morte di Madonna Laura*. While the poet's deepest anguish occurs after his lady's tragic death, his earlier poetry also demonstrates the deep physical and psychological effects of *amor hereos*. In *rima* 164, for example, Petrarca pictures himself in bed, unable to sleep and anguished by his tormented thoughts of Laura:

>Or che 'l ciel e la terra e 'l vento tace,
et le fere e gli augelli il sonno affrena,
notte il carro stellato in giro mena,
et nel suo letto il mar senz'onda giace,
>   vegghio, penso, ardo, piango; e chi mi sface
sempre m'è innanzi per mia dolce pena:
guerra è 'l mio stato, d'ira e di duol piena;
et sol di lei pensando ò qualche pace.
>   Così sol d'una chiara fonte viva
move 'l dolce et l'amaro ond'io mi pasco,
una man sola mi risana e punge;
>   et perché 'l mio martir non giunga a riva,
mille volte il dì moro e mille nasco,
tanto da la salute mia son lunge. (254)

(Now that the heavens, earth, and wind are silent
and sleep has beast and bird in its control,
while night is driving round her car of stars
and in its bed the sea rests wavelessly;
  awake, I think, burn, weep; and who destroys me
is always in my mind to my sweet pain:
war is my state, I'm full of grief and anger—

only the thought of her gives me some peace.
So from one clear and living font alone
there springs the sweet and bitter that I feed on;
one hand alone can heal and wound me both;
and that my suffering may never end
I'm born and die a thousand times a day,
so far away from my salvation. [255])

After Laura's death, Petrarca's dreams become his only link with the young woman's memory, as her phantasm continues to appear in the poet's troubled imagination in *rima* 341:

Deh, qual pietá, qual angel fu sì presto,
a portar sopra 'l cielo il mio cordoglio?
ch'ancor sento tornar pur come soglio
Madonna in quel suo atto dolce onesto,
 ad acquetare il cor misero et mesto,
piena sì d'umiltà, vota d'argoglio,
e 'n somma tal ch'a morte i' mi ritoglio,
et vivo, e 'l viver più non m'è molesto.
 Beata s'è, che pò beare altrui
co la sua vista, o ver co le parole
intellette da noi soli ambedui.
 "Fedel mio caro, assai di te mi dole;
Ma pur per nostro ben dura ti fui,"
dice, e cos'altre d'arrestare il sole. (474)[5]

(What a pity, ah, what angel was so swift
to carry through the heavens my heart's grief?
Again I fell, as in the past, returning,
my lady in her own way chaste and sweet
 to bring peace to my sad and wretched heart;
full of humility, empty of pride
she is, such that I now draw back from death
and live, and living is no longer hard.
 Blessèd is she who can make others blest
by seeing her, or with those words of hers
that only for the two of us had meaning:
 "My dear and faithful one, I grieve for you;
but for our own good I was cruel to you,"
she says, and more, enough to stay the sun. [475])

---

5. See also *rime* 219, 279, 284, 285, 319, 342, 345, 359, and 362.

Although most stilnovist poetry deals with the passions and suffering of young men, Boccaccio's *L'elegia di Madonna Fiammetta* demonstrates that the same amorous process also occurs in young women. Fiammetta first sees her beloved Panfilo during a holiday celebration, and although she observes him only briefly, his image is immediately imprinted upon her lovesick memory: "E giá nella mia mente essendo l'effigie della sua figura rimasa, non so con che tacito diletto meco la riguardava, e quasi con piú argomenti affermate vere le cose che di lui mi pareano, contenta d'essere da lui riguardata, talvolta cautamente se esso mi riguardasse mirava" (10) ("Since his image was already imprinted upon my mind, I observed it within myself with a certain quiet delight as if I were adducing new reasons to confirm the judgment I had made of him" [10]). Although Panfilo's *effigie* has already entered her imagination, Fiammetta foolishly gives way to her amorous desires and renews the visual contact with the young man.[6] She is immediately captivated by Panfilo's image, and she begins to suffer the sighs, groans, and sleepless nights that are a normal part of love melancholy.

Fiammetta and Panfilo soon start a passionate romance that ends when the young man returns to his hometown. Suddenly deprived of her lover's company, Fiammetta's erotic melancholy causes her to see the vision of Panfilo in the form of phantasy: "Io alcuna volta meco medesima fingeva lui dovere ancora, indietro tornando, venirmi a vedere, e quasi come se venuto fosse, gli occhi all'uscio della mia camera rivolgeva, e rimanendo dal mio consapevole immaginamento beffata, cosí ne rimaneva crucciosa come se con veritá fossi stata ingannata" (46) ("At times I pretended to myself that he had returned and was coming to see me again, so I turned my eyes toward the door of my room as if he had really come, and fooled by my conscious fantasy, I was thus left sulking as if I had been deceived with the truth" [42]). Fiammetta spends her evenings either thinking of Panfilo or suf-

---

6. Lovesickness is transmitted through the eyesight because according to classical as well as Renaissance theory, the eyes emit a small stream of light that creates the sense of vision. In addition, according to Marsilio Ficino, the *pneuma*, or spirit, that links the body and the soul is made up of a sanguine vapor that is also emitted with the eyesight when the lover establishes visual contact with the beloved. This sanguine vapor is created in the lover's heart, so as it enters the beloved's eyes it seeks its natural home in the *amada*'s heart. Once the *pneuma* reaches the second heart it is condensed back into blood. Nevertheless, since lovesickness is a disease of the blood, it infects the beloved with the same illness. As a result, each lover will seek visual contact with the other so that the blood they receive through the *pneuma* can be returned to the heart that originally produced it. Based on the *pneuma*'s physical qualities, Ficino concludes that erotic melancholy is transmitted in the same way as any other contagious disease (1944, part VII, 224). See further discussion of Ficino's ideas in Chapter 2.

fering from unusual dreams (73, 67), and she finds herself beckoning sleep in an attempt to recapture the young man's image in her sensual, nighttime imagination: "E nel modo usato alle lagrime ritornando, miseramente piango, e isforzandomi poi di dare alla mente riposo, con gli occhi chiusi allettando gli umidi sonni, tra me medesima in cotal guisa gli chiamo" (76) ("And I keep weeping miserably as I return to my usual tears, but then, in an effort to give my mind a rest, I close my eyes, inviting moist dreams, and calling sleep to invade me" [70]).

Boccaccio's most extensive treatment of the theme of the *inamorato*'s lovesick dream occurs in the *Amorosa visione*, a lyrical work of fifty cantos written in *terzina* verse. Virtually the entire work is made up of the poet's extended dream sequence, as indicated by the first lines of the opening sonnets:

> Mirabil cosa forse la presente
> vision vi parrà, donna gentile,
> a riguardar, sì per lo nuovo stile,
> sì per la fantasia ch'è nella mente. (1–4)

> (A wondrous thing to behold, perhaps, the present
> vision will seem to You, noble lady,
> as much for its new style,
> as for the phantasy stored in my mind. [1–4])

Boccaccio writes that love has revealed a vision to his imprisoned soul, and that with his troubled thoughts, "ch'uscita fuor di sé la fantasia / subito corse 'n non usato errore" (11–12) ("my phantasy, issuing forth from itself, / at once coursed into unfamiliar error"). In the midst of this lovelorn contemplation, the poet is overcome by the "sonno sì dolce e soave" (17) ("a sleep so sweet and gentle") of a beautiful young woman who serves as his guide during the scenes of this amorous dream.

Most of Boccaccio's vision deals with a series of love affairs, and it ends with the overpowering image of his own lady's phantasm. Nevertheless, although the poet thinks that he finally has the good fortune to have her "al mio piacere / tutta disposta" (39–40) ("completely disposed / to my pleasure"), the emotion of his unbounded joy suddenly awakens him from his dream:

> Tutto stordito mi riscossi allora
> e strinsi a me le braccia, e mi credea
> madonna in mezzo d'esse avervi ancora.

> Oimè, quanto angosciosa e quanto rea
> mi fu cotal partita, e quanto caro
> mi fu 'l dormir mentre 'n braccio v'avea! . . .
>   La fantasia non so come m'errava,
> ché, mentre avea sognato, mi credeva
> sogno non fosse e ver esser stimava. (46–52, 58–60)

> (Quite stunned, I roused myself then,
> drew my arms back to myself, thinking
> I still held the lady between them.
>   Alas, how transformed into bitter pain
> was that pleasure which sleep had brought me,
> giving remedy to my grievous woes! . . .
>   I don't know how my phantasy could have been so mistaken
> that while I had been dreaming I thought
> it was no dream and judged it to be true.)

A similar poetic dream and accompanying analysis of the psychological phenomenon of erotic melancholy appear in Lorenzo de' Medici's sonnet 19, in which *Il magnifico* asks Love for a *triegua* from the nighttime sighs and emotional suffering over his lady. In return, Lorenzo promises that he will allow Love to share the experience of the imaginary presence of his beloved, as she will appear in a vision with her beautiful face, attractive voice, and the white hand that is so dear to his heart:

> Datemi pace omai, sospiri ardenti,
> o pensiero sempre nel bel viso fissi,
> ché qualche sonno placido venissi
> alle roranti mie luci dolenti!
>   Or li uomini e le fere hanno le urgenti
> fatiche e' dur' pensiero queti e remissi,
> e già i bianchi cavalli al giogo ha missi
> la scorta de' febei raggi orienti.
>   Deh, facciàn triegua, Amor! ch'io ti prometto
> ne' sonni sol veder quello amoroso
> viso, udir le parole ch'ella dice,
>   toccar la bianca man che il cor m'ha stretto.
> O Amor, del mio ben troppo invidioso,
> lassami almen dormendo esser felice! (154)

> (Give me some peace, at last, you ardent sighs,
> And thoughts, fixed always on that lovely face,

> So that a little placid sleep may come
> To these bedewed and sorrowing lights of mine!
>   Now men and beasts enjoy from their hard thoughts
> And pressing work remission and surcease,
> The escort, too, of Phoebus' orient rays
> Has yoked already both his horses white.
>   Ah, let us make a truce, Love! for I swear
> To see none but that amorous face in dreams,
> To listen just to words she utters, and
>   To touch her white hand that has pressed my heart.
> O Love, too envious of my well being
> At least let me be happy when I sleep! [155])

Il magnifico's comments on this sonnet confirm that there is no fundamental difference between the fictional elements of lyrical expression and the apparently factual basis of his lovesick condition. Lorenzo writes that the effects of malignant humors and thoughts are particularly powerful during the evening hours and that these harmful effects are found as much in spiritual illnesses as in physical ailments:

> Sogliono comunemente tutte le infermità corporale nel sopravenire della notte pigliare augumento e affliggere più lo infermo; e questo adviene ché, mancando la virtù del sole, el quale è propizio all'umana natura, li umori maligni prendono maggiore forza e la virtù fa manco resistenzia, perché naturalmente la notte gli è data per riposo. . . . Questo medesime adviene della infirmità dello animo nostro, le quali sono nutrite da' maligni e malinconico pensieri, come le corporali da maligni umori. (154, 156)

> (Ordinarily, all the infirmities of the body, by usually arriving in the night, make the infirm worse and afflict them more. And this happens because, in the absence of the virtue of the sun, which is propitious for human nature, the malign humors gain greater power, and one's vital force makes less resistance, because the night is naturally given to it for repose. . . . The same thing happens in the infirmities of our minds, which are fed by malign and melancholy thoughts, as bodily infirmities are by malignant humors. [155, 157])

According to these comments, the lovelorn suffering of sighs and tears is not the result of any contemporary poetic convention, but is instead caused by an *infermità dello animo* that most affects the *inamorato* in the evening for primarily physiological reasons. Lorenzo believes that each of the four bodily humors controls the organism for six hours of the day.[7] The melancholic humor of black bile is in movement during the last three hours of the day and the first three hours of the evening, after which the phlegm is in movement for another six hours. Since "l'umore maninconico e flemmatico generano nella mente nostra malinconici e tristi pensieri, di necessità conviene questi tali pensieri abbino maggior forza in quello tempo che si muovono quelli umori" (156) ("the melancholic and phlegmatic humors generate in our minds melancholy and sad thoughts, of necessity it follows that such thoughts as these have greater power in that time when these humors are moving" [157]). In addition, the lovesick dreamer cannot distract himself with happier thoughts while he sleeps, and as a result the "notturni pensieri essere molto più veementi, e, quando sono maligni, molto più molesti, e per essere più potenti e per avere manco resistenzia e remedio" (156) ("nocturnal thoughts are much more vehement, and, when they are malign, much more grievous, both from being more powerful and from [our] having less resistance and remedy" [157]).

According to *Il magnifico*, the dreams that he will experience while asleep represent both a relief from and a natural extension of the "malinconici pensieri" (156) ("melancholy thoughts" [157]) and the "pensiere amorosi" (158) ("amorous thoughts" [159]) that dominate his mental process during the day. The only difference between his thought process while awake and while asleep is that his dreams represent a happier experience for him because they allow him to maintain the illusion of his beloved's physical presence:

> E però, pensando quello che più potessi fare, mi accorsi che la cagione vera del male mio, quella che moveva le lacrime, e sospiri e i pensieri, era Amore; e però cominciai a voltare a lui

---

7. According to Hippocrates, the human body contains four humors or bodily fluids: blood, phlegm, yellow bile, and black bile. Good health depends on the perfect balance of all four humors, whereas pain is caused by a humoral deficiency or excess or simply by an inappropriate combination of the humors (11, 13). Hippocrates believes that when the body loses too much of a particular humor, this "emptying causes pain" (13). Nevertheless, he insists on the differences between the four humors and does not believe that blood causes a buildup of black bile. Although medieval humoral theory is derived from classical sources, Mary Frances Wack has noted that the relationship between the humors and erotic melancholy was developed in early modern Europe (8). See also Klibansky, Panofsky, and Saxl 1964, part I, chapter 1.1, "The Doctrine of the Four Humors," 3–15; and Fraker 1993.

e miei prieghi, e, avendo chiesto a quelli primi invano pace, mi ridussi con Amore a domandarli triegua: cosa che più facilmente doveva consentire, perché la pace è una perpetua quiete, la triegua temporanea. E perché più facilmente me la consentisse, promissi ad Amore che, ancora che io dormissi, non mi rebellerei del suo regno, e ne' sonni miei vederei el viso della donna mia, udirei le sue dolce parole e toccherei quella candidissima mano; e i pensieri miei, dormendo sarebbono amorosi come erano nella vigilia, solamente con questa differenzia: che, vigilando, o per gelosia o per desiderio, e pensieri erono molestissimi e duri; dormendo, sarebbono dolci e suavi, perché adempierei quello desiderio che avevo di vedere, udire e toccare la donna mia. (160)

(And therefore, thinking about what else I could do, it occurred to me that the true cause of my ill, that which moved the tears, and the sighs and the thoughts, was Love. And therefore I began to address my prayers to him, and, having asked those first in vain for peace, I was reduced to asking for a truce with Love: a thing to which he ought easily to consent, because peace is a perpetual tranquillity, but a truce only temporary. And so he might more readily agree to it, I promised Love that, even if I slept, I would not rebel against his reign, and that in my sleep I would see the face of my lady, would hear her sweet words and would touch that very white hand. And my sleeping thoughts would be as amorous as were my waking ones, only with this difference: that, waking, either because of jealousy or desire, my thoughts were most grievous and hard; sleeping, they would be sweet and soft, because my desire would be fulfilled in seeing, hearing, and touching my lady. [161])

As revealed by the writings of Andreas, Héloïse, Dante, and Lorenzo de' Medici, there appears to be little difference between the lovesick behavior found in the life and the literature of medieval Europe. The dreams and the fantasies that appear in the *De Amore*, Héloïse's letters, Provençal poetry, and Italian prose and verse of the *duecento* and the *trecento* represent authentic manifestations of erotic melancholy that occur in both fictional and nonfictional work.[8] More important,

---

8. While the phantasmic appearance of the beloved does not seem to have been widespread in Spain, Julian Palley has found examples of this phenomenon in two medieval romances. Rabbi Sem Tob writes in the *proverbios morales:* "En sueños una fermosa / besava una vegada, / estando muy medrosa / de los de su posada. / Fallé su boca sabrosa,

this tradition was so common in European literature that there can be little doubt that Rojas and the other Celestinesque authors were well aware of this convention. For this reason, these authors would not be at all surprised by the presence of the dreamlike symptoms of lovesickness in the opening scene of *Celestina*, and they would naturally transfer comparable behavior to their rewriting of the story of Calisto and Melibea.

While *Celestina* contains repeated references to Calisto's dreamlike nature, perhaps the clearest example of these phantasies occurs at the beginning of the interpolated acts of the *Tragicomedia*. When the *galán* returns home with Sosia and Tristán in Act XIV after his first evening in Melibea's garden, he sends the two servants to bed and reveals that he prefers to spend his time in the silence of his darkened bedroom: "¡O mesquino yo, quánto me es agradable de mi natural la soledad y silencio y escuridad" (XIV, 288). Calisto then defends his actions and his honor during an imaginary conversation before an unnamed judge, but he soon realizes that the entire exchange with the judge has been another dream or vision: "Pero, ¿qué digo; con quién hablo; estoy en mi seso? ¿Qué es esto, Calisto; soñavas, duermes o velas; estáis en pie o acostado? Cata que estás en tu cámara" (XIV, 290).

Calisto decides to continue his passionate love affair with Melibea by spending his days in his bedroom and his evenings in the *paraýso dulce* of the young woman's garden (XIV, 292), but since the twelve-hour wait for nightfall seems absolutely interminable, he once again recalls the young woman's image in the form of phantasy: "¿Qué me aprovecha a mí que dé doze horas el relox de hierro si no las ha dado el del cielo? Pues por mucho que madrugue no amanesce más aýna. Pero tú, dulce ymaginación, tú que puedes me acorre; trae a mi fantasía la presencia angélica de aquella ymagen luziente; buelve a mis oýdos el suave son de sus palabras" (XIV, 292).

The *galán*'s call for his memory and his imagination in Act XIV is clearly reminiscent of Melibea's fantastic presence in *Celestina*'s opening scene, as Calisto's *fantasía* will once again bring the young

---

/ saliva muy temprada, / non vi tan dulce cosa: / mas agra a la dexada" (qtd. in Palley 72). In *El enamorado y la muerte*, the lover sees his beloved in his dreams just before death comes to claim him: "Un sueño soñaba anoche, / soñito del alma mía, / soñaba con mis amores / que mis brazos los tenía. / Vi entrar una señora tan blanca / muy más que la nieve fría. / ¿Por dónde has entrado, amor? / ¿Cómo has entrado, mi vida? / Las puertas están cerradas, / ventanas y celosías. / —No soy el amor, amante, / la Muerte que Dios te envía. / —Ay Muerte, tan rigurosa, / déjame vivir un día! / —Un día no puede ser, / una hora tienes de vida" (qtd. in Palley 36). See also Christopher Maurer's study of erotic dreams in the sixteenth- and seventeenth-century Spanish sonnet.

woman's *ymagen luziente* to his chamber.[9] And since the young lover's amorous vision represented a fantastic mix of life and literature in medieval and Renaissance Europe, it is unsurprising that the most accurate description of Calisto's condition is found in Francisco López de Villalobos's gloss to his translation of the *Anfitrión* (1544), a commentary that represents a literal combination of fictional and scientific opinions.[10] Villalobos—the personal physician to both Fernando el Católico and the emperor Carlos V—reveals that the woman's phantasy typically dominates not only the young lover's daytime thoughts and imagination, but also his dreams up to the moment of awakening:

> Entre las potencias y sentidos interiores hay una que se llama imaginativa . . . [que] es maestra de hacer imágenes y componerlas. . . . Esta imaginativa adolesce algunas veces de un género de locura que se llama alienación, y es por parte de algún malo y rebelde humor que ofusca y enturbia el espíritu do se hacen las imágenes, fórmase allí la imagen falsa . . . [y] si la tiene, es mentirosa y enajenada la imaginación, y cuanto piensa, todo es del metal de aquella imagen que allí está, de aquello habla el alienado, y en ello está rebatado y trasportado de tal manera, que no oye ni ve ni entiende cosa que le digan. . . . Los enamorados son desta materia: que la imagen de su amiga tienen siempre figurada y fija dentro de sus pensamientos, por donde no pueden ocupar jamás la imaginación en otra cosa; en esta imagen . . . están trasportados y rebatados todas las horas; con ella hablan,

---

9. Garci-Gómez (1994) notes that Melibea calls Calisto a "loco, saltaparedes, fantasma de noche, luego como cigüeña, figura de paramiento malpintado" (IV, 162). Garci-Gómez correctly concludes that Melibea's complaint suggests that the young woman—who is also affected by erotic melancholy—likewise sees nocturnal visions of Calisto: "Es decir, el Calisto que de manera normal, según Pármeno, había entrado—no saltado—por la puerta, de día—*el otro día*—, en la huerta de Melibea en pós de su neblí perdido, se le aparecía a ésta como un fantasma que asaltaba, de noche, las paredes de su castidad, luego como cigüeña, esas aves que en el folclore alemán causan con su pico el embarazo de las mujeres, las mismas que en un folclore muy generalizado son portadoras de bebés" (36). For Melibea's lovesickness, see also my *Calisto's Dream* (110–15).

10. Coincidentally, Villalobos started to write at the University of Salamanca at about the same time that Rojas would have been completing *Celestina*. According to Adolfo de Castro, "La primera de [sus obras] fue una que se intitula *Sumario de la medicina, en romance trovado, con un tratado sobre las pestíferas bulas, por el licenciado Villalobos, estudiante de Salamanca, hecho a contemplación del muy magnífico e ilustre señor el marqués de Astorga.* (Salamanca, a expensas de Antonio de Barreda, librero, año de 1498)" (xxii).

> della cantan y della lloran, con ella comen y duermen y despiertan. (488–89)

López de Villalobos thus confirms that melancholic dreams were an accepted medical as well as fictional phenomenon in Renaissance Spain. According to the professional opinion that López de Villalobos presents in his gloss to the *Anfitrión*, it would be perfectly normal for an already enamored Calisto to suddenly awaken from an imaginary conversation with his beloved Melibea at the beginning of *Celestina*. Although Calisto's dream or vision may appear unusual or perhaps illogical for modern *Celestina* scholars, contemporary readers would realize that the opening dream represents the precise behavior one would expect from a young man suffering from the effects of love melancholy.

Despite the extensive presence of lovesick dreams in European letters from the twelfth to the seventeenth centuries, we cannot say with certainty that the *antiguo auctor* used the *Paulus*, the *De Amore*, or any other specific works as the precise source texts for the phantastic vision in *Celestina*'s first scene. Nevertheless, all of the works cited above reflect a common intellectual, cultural, and literary heritage that existed throughout medieval and Renaissance Europe. There is little doubt that the dreams of erotic melancholy were considered a documented, verifiable physiological phenomenon for centuries, which would explain why Fernando de Rojas and later Celestinesque authors concluded that Melibea appeared in the first act of *Celestina* as a phantasmal presence in Calisto's lovesick dream.

2

De dónde son los fantasmas

Dream Theory from Plato to the Renaissance

In Chapter 1 of this study I analyze the history and development of lovesick dreams in European letters, a literary and social phenomenon that foreshadows Calisto's amorous vision of Melibea at the beginning of *Celestina*. Although the first chapter reveals that lovesick dreams are one of the most common manifestations of erotic melancholy in medieval and Renaissance Europe, it is important to note that the authors cited above typically do not write about young lovers' nightmares or about their unusual nighttime thoughts, but rather about sensual dreams in which the realistic yet illusory image of the beloved appears in the *inamorato*'s feverish imagination. Because of the central role of phantasmal visions in these works on erotic melancholy, here I will examine the evolution of European dream theory and the precise significance of these dreamworld images from the classical period up to the Renaissance.

Using the writings of philosophers, theologians, scholars, and medical doctors, in this chapter I will study the physiological and psychological factors that explain why lovesick dreamers such as Calisto see their beloved's image in the form of phantasy. At the same time, I will examine the relationship between the somatic processes that were thought to produce dreams, and the many traditional theories on the workings of sense perception and the human imagination.[1] Finally, I will analyze the phenomenon of lovesick dreams through the centuries and will consider how different writers and scholars might interpret and explain Calisto's opening dream.

Plato, who did not study sleep and dreams extensively, wrote one very influential passage on this subject in *The Republic* (9.571–72). Plato indicates that all men possess unnecessary desires, but these base instincts are controlled externally by the system of laws, and internally by positive desires that are reinforced by the use of reason. While the intellectual and moral qualities of the rational soul normally dominate the passions and desires of the animal soul, this controlling mechanism may be lost during slumber because the rational faculty becomes inactive while the person is asleep.[2] As a result of the rational soul's loss of control over physical desires during slumber, the animal soul's passions may dominate the dreamer's nighttime imagination. Plato therefore writes that "[t]hose [who] are aroused during sleep" experience this sensation "whenever the rest of the soul, the reasonable, gentle, and ruling part, is slumbering: whereas the wild and animal part, full of food and drink, skips about, casts off sleep, and seeks to find a way to its gratification" (220).

Plato's analysis of emotion-filled dreams—which would include Calisto's passionate visions of Melibea—establishes a pattern that is followed by European and Arabic dream theorists for almost two millennia. The philosopher believes that anyone who is dominated by his passions will be guilty of even greater excesses in his sleep, a sensual quality that is especially noticeable if these desires are sexual in nature: "[T]here is nothing [the soul] will not dare to do at that time, free of any control by shame or prudence. It does not hesitate, as it thinks, to

---

1. For important book-length studies on dreams and European dream theory, see Kruger, Agamben, and Dulaey.
2. Plato's division of the soul into three different parts influenced Arabic scholars as well as Neoplatonic Renaissance writers. Under this system, each section of the soul is endowed with a specific kind of love. The vegetative or lowest part of the soul is made up of the nutritive faculty, the faculty of growth, and the faculty of procreation. This region of the soul feels a love and attraction for nourishment and procreation, assuring the body's growth and the survival of the species. The animal part of the soul is related to external and internal sense perception, as well as to the imagination and sexual intercourse. The proximity of the soul's three different faculties ennobles the two lower faculties through their proximity to the rational soul, so this third and highest part of the soul and its intellectual faculty will, for example, influence and strengthen the animal part of the soul and its faculties of sense perception and imagination.

attempt sexual intercourse with a mother or anyone else—man, god, or beast" (220). The reasonable man, on the other hand, does not suffer from passionate dreams, because he cultivates his wisdom while awake, and as a result of this intellectual development his intellect strives to reach new areas of knowledge even while he sleeps. Plato thus distinguishes between spiritual and intellectual dreams on the one hand and passionate and physical dreams on the other, a dichotomy that exists well into the Middle Ages and the Renaissance. Because of this distinction, Calisto's sensual visions will always be regarded as a lower form of dreaming that is subject to continual criticism and censure.

Plato writes very little about sleep and dreams; Aristotle is far more influential in the development of European dream theory through his three essays on the nature and causes of sleep and dreams: "On Sleep," "On Dreams," and "On Divination in Sleep." According to Aristotle, although we naturally exercise the faculty of sense perception while awake, sleep represents the complete negation of this faculty. Aristotle believes that each of the five senses possesses a specific perceptive quality, so, for example, sight has the capacity to see physical objects, while hearing perceives a variety of external sounds. Despite this sentient ability, however, the senses alone cannot comprehend and interpret all of the external stimuli they receive. The body therefore has a controlling sensory organ, or *pneuma*, near the heart that regulates the five senses and discerns and deciphers all the information that the body sees, hears, feels, tastes, and touches.

Although slumber prevents the full use of the senses and of the body's faculty of sense perception, the heart controls the blood flow and the body's internal movements whether one is awake or asleep. Aristotle believes that all food and drink is converted into blood during digestion, a process that results in an increase in internal temperature. Since heat tends to rise in the body—corresponding to the physical properties of the element of fire—the effects of alcohol and warm food ascend directly to the head. The body therefore counteracts the sudden increase in its internal temperature by cooling the head and sending the heat downwards, a change that produces sleep and dreams: "Hence it is that men sink down when the heat which tends to keep them erect (man alone, among animals, being naturally erect) is withdrawn; and this, when it befalls them, causes unconsciousness, and afterwards imagination" (1:727).

Since the blood and the bodily fluids convey the heat of the food and drink throughout the organism, Aristotle's theories about the composition of human blood are an important part of his analysis of the physiological changes that occur during sleep. The philosopher writes that there are two kinds of blood, the "finest and purest blood... contained in the head," along with "the thickest and most turbid... [found] in the lower parts" of the body (1:727). As food and drink are absorbed into the bloodstream during normal digestion, this sanguinary segregation is disturbed because the purest part of the blood loses its natural, unadulterated quality. Nevertheless, the digestion again separates the two kinds of blood while the person sleeps, and then returns them to the appropriate part of the body. The sleeper awakens when digestion is complete and the blood fully segregated.

In his analysis of dreams, Aristotle writes that the five senses receive no direct, external stimulation while the person is asleep; this means that dreams correspond entirely to the faculty of imagination because they have no real connection to the temporarily inoperative senses. Although the five senses are absent while the person is sleeping, the dreamer may think that he detects external stimuli, because the imagination retains the memory of objects previously perceived while awake. Moreover, Aristotle writes that human emotions are more powerful during sleep because the senses and the intellect cannot function as controlling mechanisms to rein in these unbridled passions. As a result, an individual who goes to bed while governed by his emotions is likely to have this ardent state reflected in his dreams, as evidenced by the lover who sees the image of his beloved while sleeping:

> [L]et us now assume... that even when the external object of perception has departed, the impressions it has made persist, and are themselves objects of perception; and let us assume, besides, that we are easily deceived respecting the operations of sense-perception when we are excited by emotions... for example... the amorous person by amorous desire; so that, with but little resemblance to go upon... he sees the object of his desire; and the more deeply one is under the influence of the emotion, the less similarity is required to give rise to these impressions. (1:732)

While Aristotle believes that the dreamworld imagination is linked to the individual's emotional state, he also indicates that dreams are controlled by the physiological changes that take place during slumber. The philosopher writes that heat moves from the exterior of the body to the interior while the person is sleeping, and that the displaced heat creates an internal motion that distorts the images that occur in dreams. Just as an image reflected in a liquid is deformed if the fluid is disturbed in any way, "in the same manner during sleep the images . . . which are based upon the sensory impressions, become sometimes quite obliterated by the above described motion" (1:733). Nevertheless, as the blood becomes separated and calm during sleep through the process of digestion, the distortion of the images ceases, and the phantasms and sounds created by the imagination become so distinct and lifelike that the dreamer erroneously concludes that this false information is authentic: "[A]s the blood becomes calm and separated the fact that the movement, based on impressions derived from each of the organs of sense, is preserved in its integrity, renders the dreams coherent, causes an image to present itself, and makes the dreamer think . . . that he actually sees, and owing to those which come from the organ of hearing, that he really hears; and so on with those also which proceed from the other sensory organs" (1:733).

Although Aristotle writes that dreamers believe that they see and hear external sights and sounds during slumber, this sentient stimulation is clearly misleading because the five senses remain at rest while the person is asleep. As noted above, Aristotle indicates that the senses are governed by a "controlling sensory organ" that discerns and interprets the information received by the five senses (1:723). Since the philosopher believes that the body's internal movement of blood and heat stimulates the eyes, the ears, and the other senses—and since during sleep the inert senses cannot contradict these internally-generated perceptions with real, external stimuli—then the controlling sensory organ mistakenly concludes that the body is seeing and hearing the sights and sounds that correspond to genuine images.

Because of the effects of the body's internal movements on the five senses, the sleeper's dreamworld consciousness thinks that the false apparitions that appear in the dreamer's imagination represent authentic, external phenomena. Significantly, Aristotle indicates that the deceptive experience of dream images is particularly common at the moment of awakening. As noted above, the philosopher writes that the digestion of food and drink leaves the blood calm and fully separated toward the end of sleep. Since the undisturbed bodily liquids create images that are especially accurate and realistic, dreamers, "in the moment of awakening, surprise the images which present themselves . . . in sleep, and find that they are really but movements lurking in the organs of sense" (1:734).

While modern readers might conclude that the ability to see phantasms is an insignificant mental process, Aristotle and other classical scholars believe that the internalized image is the soul's very basis of knowledge. Aristotle writes that the only way that the thinking part of the soul perceives external events is through images either received by the senses or created by the imagination: "To the thinking soul images serve as if they were contents of perception (and when it asserts or denies them to be good or bad it avoids or pursues them). That is why the soul never thinks without an image" ("On the Soul," 1:685). It is also important to note that Aristotle, much like Plato, concludes that the soul and the body share emotions and sensual perceptions, so imaginary visions have the ability to affect the soul as much as they affect the body.

There are several parts of Aristotle's study of sleep and dreams that explain why Calisto would perceive the false image of Melibea's apparition in *Celestina*'s first scene. In the first place, Aristotle writes that dreams are the internal recollection of external images already known to the dreamer, just as the likeness of Melibea is known to the lovesick Calisto. This illusion of a corporeal presence is caused by the movement of heat and blood in the body, a physical activity that stimulates the eyes and produces an internal simulation of sight. Second, Aristotle believes that the emotions have free rein over the dreamworld imagination because the intellect is dormant during sleep. A lovelorn young man such as Calisto would be very likely to see the vision of his beloved while sleeping because his emotions would not be subject to the control of his rational faculties. Last, Aristotle indicates that realistic dreams often occur during the early morning hours—the precise time that Calisto dreams about Melibea at the start of *Celestina*—because the blood is calm and separated and the resulting images more clearly defined.

Since Aristotle believes that dreams are produced by an identifiable physiological process, he rejects the widely accepted idea that dreams have the ability to foretell the future. Nevertheless, in contrast to Aristotle's position on the mundane character of these dreams, most classical writers believe that at least some dreamworld visions are caused by spiritual and divine factors. For example, as Steven F. Kruger has noted, Synesius of Cyrene (c. 370–414) takes a completely contrary stance to Aristotle, concluding that the dream visions that appear to man reveal higher truths that are hidden from his normal thought processes (19).

Unlike Aristotle and Synesius, who adopt contrary positions on the mundane or spiritual nature of dreams, most classical scholars take an intermediate position between these two extremes.[3] Later Latin authors

---

3. Iamblichus (died c. 330 B.C.), for example, believes that internally generated dreams occur in persons "excited by the soul, or by some of our conceptions, or by rea-

continue this tradition of analyzing worldly as well as spiritual visions. Of these commentators, the most influential for medieval and Renaissance writers are Macrobius, author of the *Commentary on the Dream of Scipio*,[4] and Calcidius, who wrote the *Commentary on Plato's Timaeus*. *Scipio's Dream* is the sixth and final book of Cicero's *De republica*, and is—with the exception of some brief textual fragments—the only section of the work known in western Europe until the nineteenth century. The most important part of Macrobius's *Commentary* related to dream theory is chapter 3 of book 1, in which he "describe[s] the many varieties of dreams recorded by the ancients" (1.3.87).

Macrobius writes that the lowest and most mundane kind of dream is the nightmare, called *insomnium* in Latin and *enypnion* in Greek. These deceptive visions are caused by physical or mental distress, and are related to normal daily problems. Macrobius indicates that among the kinds of nightmares caused by physical distress are those resulting from excessive eating or drinking, while as "examples of the mental variety, we might mention the lover who dreams of possessing his sweetheart or of losing her" (1.3.88). The second but higher form of mundane dream is the apparition, called *visum* in Latin and *phantasma* in Greek. This false dream occurs just before the moment of awakening, but it is full of terrible specters that correspond to the phantoms rather than to the actual dreams found in Aristotle.

It is clear that Macrobius would explain Calisto's dream as an *insomnium* caused by the *galán*'s anguished emotional state. The spectral *visum* has no relation to the enigmatic conversation between the two future lovers in *Celestina*, even though they both take place at the same time of the day. In this sense, Macrobius diverges from Aristotle, for he believes that shortly before awakening—during what he calls "the moment between wakefulness and slumber" (1.3.89)—the imagination produces terrible visions of inhuman content. As we have seen, Aristotle indicates that just the opposite occurs: when the body is at rest, and the blood and bodily fluids lie in a tranquil state, then the early morning imagination produces its most exact and credible visions of realistic human figures.

---

son, or by imaginations, or certain diurnal cares." Iamblichus also accepts the existence of infallible, divine dreams that take place when the soul and God are united in sleep. During these externally generated, spiritual dreams, the soul "receives the most true plenitudes of intellections . . . and derives the most genuine principles of knowledge" (qtd. in Kruger 19).

4. See Stahl 42–55; Peden; Bodenham 74–75; and Silvestre for the influence of Macrobius in the Middle Ages.

Calcidius, in his *Commentary on Timaeus* (A.D. 249-56), provides a more complex hierarchical dream structure than does Macrobius. Calcidius concludes that Aristotle's belief in the exclusively mundane nature of dreams is akin to his denying the existence of a divine presence on earth. He therefore presents a Neoplatonic analysis that allows for both divine and human dreams. There are three classifications of mundane dreams in Calcidius's continuum, with two of these further divided into subcategories. First, "[t]here are [dreams] that, as though the mind has been gravely struck and beaten by the deeply imprinted vestiges of pain, revive in sleep images of past consternation." Second, there are two kinds of dreams "that arise in consequence of the rational part of the soul (a) [when it is] either pure and free from perturbation (b) or situated among passions." Third, there are divinatory and spectral dreams, which are "(a) those that are shown as predictions by divine powers looking out [for us], (b) or even those fashioned in a dreadful and horrid shape in place of a punishment [for us] because of some transgression" (qtd. in Kruger 30).

The most meaningful dream for *Celestina*'s readers is of the second classification, the vision that takes place in the rational soul. Significantly, the nature of these mundane dreams varies according to the person's mental and emotional state, so—as in Aristotle and Macrobius—this variety of dream consists of a vision that is determined by internal physical and mental phenomena. According to the dichotomy in Calcidius's reading of Plato's *The Republic*, dreams in the rational soul correspond to either moderate or intemperate thoughts and are therefore ruled by either reason or the appetite. Calcidius writes that in those dreams ruled by the human emotions, "[T]here is nothing that it [the nonrational part of the soul] may not dare to do, as though [it had been] released and freed from the precepts of virtue and modesty; for indeed, as it judges, it does not fear to embrace and lie with [the dreamer's] mother, nor does it hesitate to provoke any man or god, nor does it seem to itself to refrain from any slaughter or shameful act" (qtd. in Kruger 27).

Since Calcidius's interpretation of human dreams is clearly influenced by Plato's writings, his explanation for Calisto's amorous visions would likely follow classical models. The *galán*'s emotions have obviously overwhelmed his intellect, which means that his animal passions maintain an absolute control of his thought process during slumber. While Calisto does not attempt to "embrace and lie" with his mother—a possibility presented by Plato and repeated by Calcidius—this is precisely what he attempts to do with Melibea in his nighttime imagination. Calisto's lovesickness has impaired his use of reason, and as a result there appears to be little alternative to the sensual images that dominate the young man's dreamworld imagination.

The duality of mundane and divine dreams in Macrobius and Calcidius is vitally important for Christian writers who appropriate the scholarly learning of the classical world. These writers cannot accept Aristotle's idea that all dreams correspond to internal physical factors, because the New Testament begins with three dreams that lie at the very core of Christian beliefs.[5] The divine dream is also found in the Old Testament, which begins with a celestial intervention during sleep. Since Adam finds himself alone in Eden, the Lord God causes a deep sleep to fall over him so that he can remove Adam's rib and use it to create Eve (Gen. 2.21-22). Saint Augustine (354-430) writes on the nature and significance of this sleep in his *Two Books on Genesis Against the Manichees*, written in 388 or 389. According to Augustine, Genesis reveals that Eve was created to be Adam's helper and to establish a spiritual union between man and woman. Augustine's commentary describes a divine order in which the soul controls the body, while virile reason controls physical desires with the soul's guidance.

Since man often does not understand the difference between reason and sensual desires, Augustine concludes, God caused sleep to come over Adam so that he would see with his internal rather than his external eyes. Augustine thus believes that higher knowledge in sleep is achieved through a process that requires absolute sense deprivation: "Because he sees these things with a more hidden wisdom, I think this hidden wisdom is signified by the sleep that God sent upon Adam when he made the woman for him. To see this there is no need of these bodily eyes; rather to the extent that anyone withdraws from these visible signs into the interior realm of the intelligence (for this is in a sense to fall asleep), to the extent that he sees it better and more clearly" (1:112-13).

Augustine's analysis of Genesis describes a form of spiritual sleep that is diametrically opposed to the sensual visions experienced by

---

5. When Joseph discovers that the Virgin is bearing a child, he decides to put Mary away in private rather than make a public example of her. An angel then appears to Joseph in a dream and informs him that the unborn child was conceived by the Holy Spirit in fulfillment of the Scriptures; the angel also tells him that he must wed Mary and name the boy Jesus (Mat. 1.20-23). A second dream warns the three Wise Men to avoid returning to Herod after Jesus' birth in Bethlehem, and shortly afterward an angel of the Lord appears to Joseph and tells him to take his family to Egypt so that Herod will not kill the child (Mat. 2.12-13). In the Christian tradition, divine dreams not only announce the news of the Virgin's immaculate conception, but also are responsible for saving Jesus' life at the hands of Herod.

Calisto. In Augustine's view, Adam's divinely induced slumber teaches him a "perfect wisdom . . . so that the flesh does not lust against the spirit" (113). As a result of this divine wisdom, both Adam and Eve are naked in the Garden of Eden, but they feel no shame or embarrassment, because they are ruled by the "simplicity and chastity of [the] soul" (115). Calisto, on the other hand, experiences a mundane dream in which "la grandeza de Dios" is not symbolized by a spiritual knowledge of God (I, 85), but rather by the memory of Melibea's remarkable physical beauty. In Calisto's dream, the *galán* speaks of his misguided "devoción y obras pías que por este lugar alcançar [tiene] a Dios offrecido" (I, 86), but this devotion is ruled by Calisto's emotions and his sensual desires rather than by his reason. Considering the strength of the young man's emotional state, it is little wonder that he prefers to experience Melibea's illusory image rather than the true spiritual union with God and all of his saints in heaven (I, 87).

Augustine was interested above all in spiritual dreams and the divine knowledge that they reveal to man, but he also discusses the nature of mundane dreams in book 12 of *The Literal Meaning of Genesis* ("The Paradise or Third Heaven Seen by Saint Paul"). Reflecting the same duality that Augustine sees in the contrast between the soul and the body, he writes that human dreams deal with strictly inferior, earthly concerns. Because of the mundane nature of these dream images, Augustine indicates that they are quite different from the heavenly knowledge contained in spiritual visions:

> [I]n the ordinary course of our daily life there are . . . objects that arise in various ways from our spirit [i.e., the imaginative faculty] itself or are . . . suggested to the spirit by the body, according as we have been influenced by the flesh or by the mind. Thus men in their waking hours think of their troubles, turning over in their minds the likenesses of bodily things; and so in their sleep, too, they frequently dream of something they need. . . . [I]n my opinion, when these objects are compared with the revelations of angels, they ought to be assigned the same relative value that we give, in the corporeal order, to earthly bodies in comparison with celestial bodies. (2:221)

Augustine also examines sense perception in this section of *The Literal Meaning of Genesis*, as he underlines the importance of images in human dreams and in the acquisition of knowledge. Augustine notes that when a person reads the commandment You shall love your neighbor as yourself, this sensory process creates three different kinds of visions. The first vision is corporeal and consists of the eye's actual perception of the commandment's written words. The second vision is spiritual because the person's comprehension of this commandment creates the phantastic representation of the neighbor in the spirit or imaginative faculty. This spiritual or imaginary vision is not physical because "we see nothing with the eyes of the body but in the soul behold corporeal images" (2:185–86). Instead, the imagination perceives "the image of an absent body, though it resembles a body, is not itself a body any more than is the act of vision by which it is perceived" (2:186). Finally, there is the strictly intellectual vision of the love that is felt toward the person's neighbor, a different and higher kind of vision because "love can neither be seen in its own essence with the eyes of the body nor be thought of in the spirit by means of an image like a body; but only in the mind, that is, in the intellect, can it be known and perceived" (2:191).[6]

Although Augustine indicates that mundane dreams and visions are clearly inferior to divine ones, he also writes that dreams of sexual content are not inherently sinful. Augustine believes that even the virtuous who would never engage in actual carnal activity sometimes experience erotic dreams "because they cannot control the appearance of those corporeal images that are indistinguishable from bodies" (2:199). Nevertheless, he also thinks that it is possible for the soul to dominate the body during sleep, so not all dreamers experience these sexual visions. Augustine writes:

> [I]f the images of these corporeal things . . . were to appear in sleep as vividly as do real bodies to those who are awake, there would follow that which in waking hours could not happen without sin. . . . Moreover, when the image . . . becomes so vivid in the dream of the sleeper that it is indistinguishable from actual intercourse, it immediately moves the flesh and the natural result follows. Yet this happens without sin, just as the matter is spoken of without sin by a man wide awake, who doubtlessly thinks about it in order to speak of it. (2:198–99)

Augustine thus indicates that dreams often present the sensual image of the beloved, a possibility already considered by Plato,

---

6. As Steven F. Kruger has noted, the image is a central part of Augustine's hierarchical structure of human and divine visions (37). Like Aristotle, Augustine believes that these immaterial images are necessary for the soul—which is also immaterial—to comprehend the significance of the body's ideas and perceptions.

Aristotle, Macrobius, and Calcidius. Nevertheless, his interpretation of Calisto's amorous vision would be quite different from the one presented by classical scholars. Greek and Roman writers believe that the rational faculty is inoperative while one is asleep, but that a wise person who relies on the intellect would not be subject to sensual images while asleep. Augustine, on the other hand, would indicate that Calisto's nighttime activity is not morally wrong, because it is beyond his rational control. From a patristic perspective, Calisto's fault lies in his effort to repeat while awake the same sexual activity he dreams about night after night.

In the eighth and ninth centuries, Arabic scholars began to prepare translations and commentaries on the works of Greek physicians, philosophers, and mathematicians. The writings of Avicenna, Averroes, Rhazes, and other scholars and doctors were in turn translated into Latin during the twelfth-century Renaissance, as this combination of Arabic and Greek scholarship became the pillar of European medical and philosophical knowledge for centuries. Avicenna (980–1037), whose medical writings became standard reference works in Europe well into the Baroque period, writes extensively on the role of phantasm in the process of learning and sense perception. Avicenna holds a Neoplatonic view of love that highlights the contrast between physical and spiritual beauty. In this intellectual and metaphysical system, the highest object of human love is the divinity, while the lowest form of love is found in man's animalistic attraction for material pleasures.

When the imagination and animal desires are controlled by reason, sexual intercourse is used only for procreation and to preserve the species. As in the classical tradition, love represents a desire for beauty, but reason loves and desires a higher form of spiritual beauty divorced from its base, physical aspects. Nevertheless, despite the rational attraction for this immaterial beauty, Avicenna writes that if human passions are not subject to reason, then this adverse relationship creates the same physical attraction found in animals: "Both the rational and the animal soul—the latter by its proximity to the former—invariably love what has beauty of order, composition and harmony. . . . [I]t is part of the nature of beings endowed with reason to covet a beautiful sight. . . . But if it is specific to the animal faculty alone, the sages do not consider it as a sign of refinement and nobility. For . . . when man expresses animal desires in an animal-like fashion, he becomes involved in vice and is harmed in his rational soul" (220–21).

Although the closeness of the rational, animal, and vegetative souls normally leads to the control of the higher part of the soul over the lower parts, the opposite occurs if the imagination frees itself from the control of reason. When this happens, the imagination believes itself capable of contemplating images or "intelligible beings" that in reality are perceptible only to the rational soul (219). This confusion of spiritual and mundane elements takes place because divine perfection—which all men love and should strive to attain—appears to the human soul in the form of images. Nevertheless, the soul's imaginative faculty also generates images from memory, although these apparitions do not have a true spiritual basis as do the images perceived by the rational soul.

According to Avicenna, rational human love is also communicated from one person to another through images comprehensible only to the soul: "A rational soul acts upon another rational soul by imposing upon it its image, namely, the intelligible form" (226). This manifestation of images appears to the soul "without the assistance of sense-perception [*pneuma*] or imagination" (227) because the higher beauty of the spirit cannot be directly perceived by the faculties found in the animal soul. Despite this barrier to direct perception, however, the proximity of the rational soul causes the image to be progressively revealed to "the animal faculty ... then the vegetative faculty and then nature" (227).

Avicenna's Neoplatonic analysis of intelligible and illusory images provides another possible interpretation for Calisto's confusing vision of Melibea. Dominated by his animal passions rather than by his rational soul, the *galán* thinks that he sees the divine image of his beloved, but only the rational soul is capable of perceiving authentic spiritual images. Calisto's impassioned imagination mistakenly believes that it has assumed the soul's ability to contemplate the young woman's divine *forma*, but in fact Calisto merely visualizes the empty image of her *materia*. Since Calisto's animal faculties have rebelled against the control of reason, he does not manifest a higher, spiritual love for Melibea's immortal soul, but rather the sordid, sensual desire for the young woman's external beauty.

The works of Aristotle, Calcidius, Augustine, and Avicenna were widely read throughout medieval Europe, and the intellectual prestige of these writers influenced the development of dream theory throughout the continent. Spiritual visions continued to occupy religious writers, but other scholars showed greater interest in human dreams and their physiological causes. Medieval theory takes the predominantly Aristotelian approach that dreams correspond to internal, physical factors, but the presence of the devil in some lower dreams gives these visions a potentially evil and diabolical nature. According to the mystic abbess Hildegard of Bingen (1098–1179), for example, the devil is responsible for creating the erotic visions experienced by lovesick dreamers, and as a result of this demonic influence the phantasms that appear in sensual dreams are capable of the most sinful activity imaginable. Hildegard writes: "[W]hen sometimes [a man] falls asleep in delight of the flesh, diabolic illusion will also sometimes produce this [delight] in him [when he sleeps], in such a way that it shows to him the bodies of the living and even sometimes the bodies of the dead, with whom [the dreamer] has sometimes had familiarity of whom he truly never saw with corporeal eyes. [This happens] in such a way that it seems to him that he takes delight with them [the imagined bodies] in sins and pollutions, as though he were awake" (qtd. in Kruger 77).[7]

While writers from the classical period to the Middle Ages repeatedly describe erotic images as the lowest form of human dreams, Platonic Renaissance writers believe that love is directly responsible for the physiological changes that produce these sensual visions. According to such scholars as Marsilio Ficino (1433–99), only a spiritual relationship preserves the *inamorato*'s ethical balance, while the unloosed passions of sensual love create physical disturbances that produce the phantastic visions of erotic melancholy.[8] Ficino believes that mundane desires in a man reveal a double attraction in the lover because while the soul is drawn to his beloved's immaterial image, at the same time the senses are attracted to the woman's material presence. As in Avicenna, the soul communicates its attraction through phantasmal images, so the soul longs for the immaterial vision of the beloved when it is affected by these desires. At the same time, the physical aspect of this allurement forces the lover to search for visual contact with his *amada*, a phenomenon previously described in Chapter 1 above. According to Ficino, as the *inamorato* searches for his beloved, his "live spirits," or *pneuma*—the vital material that Ficino

---

7. The contrast between spiritual and physical love notwithstanding, some medieval writers experience dream sequences that combine both passions. According to Mary Frances Wack, "Loving compassion for the wounded, suffering body of Christ, under the guidance of the active religious imagination . . . could express itself in images of unabashed eroticism. Rupert of Deutz (d. 1129) reports a dream in which he worshipped the Cross. The crucified Christ seemed to return his gaze and accept his salutation. Yet he wanted closer union with his Savior. Rushing to the altar, he embraced and kissed the image. 'I held him, I embraced him, I kissed him for a long time. I sensed how seriously he accepted this gesture of love when, while kissing, he himself opened his mouth that I might kiss more deeply.'. . . Rupert's vision, though perhaps more vividly represented than others, is part of a medieval tradition of affective piety in which experiences of spiritual union were represented through images and gestures of loving behavior" (24–25).

8. Ficino, also known as the *alter Plato*, was the founder of Cosimo de' Medici's Platonic Academy in Florence (1462) and the originator of the Platonist revival in European letters. See Kristeller, Marcel, Ciavolella, Westra, and Wolters.

believes is made up of the purest part of the blood—exit through the eyes in order to reestablish direct contact with her.[9]

As we have seen, Aristotle indicated many centuries earlier that the body contains two kinds of blood, a purer part found in the upper body and a thicker part that resides in the lower body. According to Ficino, sensual passion causes a loss of the purest kind of blood through the *pneuma*'s, or vital spirit's, visual search for the beloved: "To whatever the serious attention of the soul is directed, to that also fly the spirits, which are the chariots or vehicles of the soul. The spirits are created in the heart from the finest part of the blood. To the image of the loved one fixed in the fancy and to the loved one himself, the soul of the lover is attracted. The spirits are drawn to the same place. Flying thither, they are quickly spent and so in order for the consumed vapors to be regenerated there must be a frequent outpouring of pure blood" (1944, part VI, 194–95).

As a result of the *pneuma*'s depletion of the purest part of the blood, Ficino concludes, the lover is left with nothing but the thickest and most corrupt part of the bloodstream. This sanguinary condition in turn creates the black bile that produces erotic melancholy, particularly in lovers such as Calisto who experience a physical attraction for their beloved:

> All of the finer and clearer parts of the blood are continually exhausted in regeneration of the spirits; therefore, since the clear and pure blood is used up, there remains only the impure, thick, dry, and black parts. Hence the body dries out and grows rough, and hence lovers become melancholy. For from the dry, thick, and black blood, melancholy, that is, black bile, is made, which fills the head with its vapors, dries out the brain, and unceasingly vexes the soul day and night with fearful, hideous images. . . . This has happened usually to those who, neglecting contemplative love, have turned to a passion for physical embrace. For we bear much more easily the desires for seeing, than those of both seeing and touching the desired one. (Ficino 1944, part VI, 194–95)

---

9. The *pneuma* is the almost immaterial essence or vapor that links the soul and the body, and that also transmits the soul's vital force to the body. Death severs the link between the eternal soul and the corruptible body, and begins the process of corporeal decay. According to Ficino, this spirit reflects the phantasms perceived by the senses, and permits the soul to contemplate these images as though they were reflected in a mirror (1944, part VI, 189). For a discussion of the development of the theory of the *pneuma*, see Couliano 4–11, 28–32.

Although throughout the centuries the dream images and uncontrolled desires of physical love are repeatedly criticized as an aberration of man's wisdom and as a corruption of his rational soul, Fernando de Rojas's Neoplatonic contemporaries in Italy believe that sensual love is also responsible for creating the somatic conditions that produce an excess of black bile by draining the body of the lightest and purest part of the blood. This surplus of dark, impure blood and black bile then causes the melancholy and the terrible mental images that often plague Calisto and other young lovers. In this Renaissance joining of dream and humoral theory—two elements that traditionally were studied separately—mundane love is analogous to a physical illness that is directly responsible for creating the phantasmal images that invade the *inamorato*'s dreamworld imagination.

Sixteenth-century writers thus return to an Aristotelian approach that highlights the physiological causes of dreams, but within a Neoplatonic structure that stresses the fundamental differences between mundane and spiritual love. According to this interpretation of lovesickness, Calisto's error is that he is interested in a purely physical relationship with Melibea. Since the young man ignores the spiritual aspects of this love, the resulting loss of *pneuma* leads to an illness that produces his erotic visions of Melibea. Calisto's opening dream is therefore not an aberration or an anomaly, but rather exactly those reactions that would be expected from a young man caught in the web of love's passions.

In the same way that Ficino combines the soul's desire for immaterial images with the physical attraction for the material presence of the beloved, medieval and Renaissance theory emphasizes that the phantasmal presence is found not only in human dreams, but also in spiritual perception. As noted above, Aristotle, Augustine, and Avicenna believe that images represent the only vehicle by which the soul perceives and interprets external information, and this combination of classical, patristic, and Arabic wisdom was widely accepted in medieval Europe. Nevertheless, in the Renaissance conception, the *pneuma*, or spirit, that links the body and the soul reflects the images captured by the five senses, which allows the soul to perceive the image of this external stimuli. As Ioan Couliano writes,

> [T]he body opens up to the soul a window to the world through the five sensory organs whose messages go to the same cardiac apparatus which . . . is engaged in codifying them so that they may become comprehensible. Called *phantasia* or inner sense [i.e., Aristotelian sense perception], the sidereal spirit transforms

messages from the five senses into *phantasms* perceptible to the soul. For the soul cannot grasp anything that is not converted into a sequence of phantasms; in short, it can understand nothing without phantasms (*aneu phantas-matos*). This passage is rendered in Latin by William of Moerbecke, translator of Aristotle, as follows: *Numquam sine phantasmate intelligit anima*. And St. Thomas uses it almost literally in his *Summa theologica*, which was of enormous influence in the succeeding centuries: *Intelligere sine conversione ad phantasmata est (animae) praeter naturam*. (5)

During the Renaissance, European scholars and writers concluded that the soul can only perceive and understand external information through the patterns and images formed by phantasms, which also turns out to be the same visual principle that forms the basis of medieval dream theory. According to Vincent of Beauvais, for example, "[S]ine phantasmatibus non est aliquod somnium (there is no dream without apparitions)" (qtd. in Kruger 110), but this is of course the same principle that guides dream theory from the time of Plato. It is clear that these images and phantasms establish the visual link between the soul's inner perceptions on the one hand, and the physical and psychological forces that control the body's dreamworld imagination on the other.

While there are many changes in European and Arabic dream theory over two millennia, there are elements that remain constant, from ancient Greece to the Renaissance. Two of the most common are, first, the phantasmal nature of human and divine dreams, and second, the continual censure of erotic and sensual visions. For Plato, sensual dreams occur when the wild passions of the animal soul overwhelm the nighttime imagination. The wise cultivate their intellect during the day, which assures the rational soul's control over sleep and produces a search for divine visions and illumination. Aristotle emphasizes the somatic causes of dreams, but indicates that the absence of sense perception during slumber leaves the imagination as the dominant dreamworld faculty. In the case of persons governed by their emotions, however, the nighttime imagination runs wild and is responsible for the deceptive image of the object of its desire.

Macrobius studies both human and divine dreams, and he indicates that lovesick images are common examples of the *insomnium*, which is the lowest form of dream and the furthest from divine inspiration. Calcidius also examines higher and lower dreams, and accepts Plato's idea that intemperate thoughts lead to the most shocking fantasies possible, such as when the dreamer imagines that he is lying with his own mother. Augustine believes that, because of their mundane nature, human dreams are inferior to higher visions and as a result they are undeserving of the prominence accorded to divine revelations. Higher dreams teach man to avoid lust and earthly desires, whereas sensual dreams are completely divorced from heavenly inspiration. While even the chaste may experience these sensual dreams, the dreamer remains free from sin because this is an involuntary reaction that occurs during sleep.

Avicenna holds the Neoplatonic view that physical beauty is inferior to spiritual beauty, a nobler attraction that is perceived only by the rational soul. Nevertheless, during sleep the animal soul may rebel against the rational soul, which causes the spirit to lose itself in blind, animal passions. Hildegard of Bingen writes that sensual images are caused by diabolical influences that rule over lovesick dreamers, which means that these visions are characterized by depraved, lustful activity. Finally, Marsilio Ficino indicates that sensual love produces a physical illness that leads directly to melancholic and amorous visions.

According to medieval and Renaissance theories of dream formation and sense perception, Calisto's vision of Melibea appears to have both a physiological and a spiritual basis. Sensual love creates a melancholic condition in the young man that leads him to see and hear Melibea's phantasm in his lovesick imagination. His rational soul, which in an ideal Neoplatonic order would lead him to a higher, spiritual love for God, is instead infected with the animal soul's insane passions. As a result of this sensual contamination, Calisto's intellect is incapable of leading him away from his destructive material desires. Nevertheless, whether one chooses to view Calisto's love for Melibea from a Platonic, Aristotelian, patristic, Arabic, or religious point of view, one conclusion is inescapable for *Celestina*'s readers: in the work's opening scene, Calisto's sensual desire for Melibea causes the young woman's illusory image to appear in the *galán*'s dreamworld imagination in the form of phantasy.

3

Calisto's Lovesickness and the Diagnosis of Heras and Crato, *Médicos*

Celestina may be considered not only a difficult and even contradictory work, but also a series of different components or subtexts, each of which contains its own specific textual problems and complications. The first part of *Celestina* is the anonymous *Auto* or *papeles* that Fernando de Rojas found in Salamanca and used as the first and longest act of the *Comedia de Calisto y Melibea*. Since the *Auto*'s original manuscript is now lost, it is unclear if Rojas altered the primitive text in any way, or if he simply included a verbatim copy of the manuscript in the *Comedia*'s first Burgos edition of 1499. If Rojas truly completed the *Comedia* during a fifteen-day vacation—as indicated in the "El autor a un su amigo" letter from the second Toledo edition of 1500—then this would suggest that the changes he made to the primitive text were minimal. Unfortunately, it is difficult to judge the accuracy of Rojas's testimony because of the ambiguous nature of the comments in the opening letter: "Asimismo pensarían que no quinze días de unas vacaciones, mientra mis socios en sus tierras, en acabarlo me detoviesse, como es lo cierto; pero aun más tiempo y menos acepto" (70–71).

The most important aspect of recent *Auto* scholarship is Charles B. Faulhaber's discovery of a copy of a fragment of an apparently earlier version of Act I, contained in Manuscript 1520 of Madrid's Biblioteca de Palacio. The fragment represents an eight-page transcription of about half of the first act, apparently written by two different copyists, with minor corrections in a third hand.[1] Faulhaber's original study (1990) on the manuscript indicates that "[t]he copy of the *Comedia* . . . definitely dates from the first half of the 16th century and, on paleographic grounds, probably from the first quarter" (6). In a later article, however, Faulhaber (1991) concludes that the manuscript is in reality Rojas's own holograph copy of the Salamanca *papeles*, with corrections that represent the first draft of his rewriting of Act I.[2] Despite Faulhaber's preliminary conclusions, in subsequent research, Ian Michael, Michel García, and Donald McGrady present convincing arguments that the manuscript is a copy of an older transcription of the *Auto*, closer to what the primitive text might have looked like when it reached Rojas's hands.

The second and longest part of *Celestina* is Fernando de Rojas's 1499 continuation of the *Comedia*, which represents an addition of fifteen acts to the original *Auto*. As noted above, the *Comedia* of 1500 contains "El autor a un su amigo," an opening letter that explains the work's unusual genesis and that emphasizes *Celestina*'s didactic nature. The 1500 edition of the *Comedia* also includes a colophon addressed to the reader and written by Alonso de Proaza, who is identified as the "corrector de la impresión" (341). The verses of Proaza's colophon not only reveal that the name of *Celestina*'s author is found in the work's opening acrostic poem, but also indicate the way that the work should be read in public: "[F]inge leyendo mil artes y modos; / pregunta y responde por boca de todos, / llorando o riyendo en tiempo y sazón" (345).

---

1. Ian Michael writes: "Don Manuel Sánchez Mariana, jefe de la sección de manuscritos de la Biblioteca Nacional de Madrid, opina que la primera mano cortesana del siglo XVI escribió el fol. 93 y probablemente los folios 98 a 100, mientras que una segunda mano, más humanística, escribió los fols. 94 a 97. La corrección entre líneas del folio 94v es de una tercera mano" (160 n. 14).

2. According to Faulhaber, Dorothy Severin also concludes that the manuscript is "obviously a *borrador* for the entire *Comedia* in Rojas's notarial hand, with more corrections to the first act" (1991, 3). Alan Deyermond agrees with Severin that "the manuscript [is] in all probability part of Rojas' draft revision of the anonymous author's Act 1, and therefore represent[s] a half-way stage between the 'papeles' found by Rojas and the text of Act 1 printed in the 1499 *Comedia*" (20). Deyermond adds that both Ian Michael and Francisco Rico disagree with this position (20–21).

The *Tragicomedia de Calisto y Melibea* was published between 1500 and 1502, although the earliest Spanish edition now extant dates from 1507. The text of the *Tragicomedia* presents five new acts, along with numerous changes to Act I and to Rojas's continuation and opening letter. The *Tragicomedia* also contains a prologue that emphasizes life's conflictive nature and that indicates that this conflict will be reflected in each reader's differing background and unique approach to the text: "Assí que quando diez personas se juntaren a oír esta comedia en quien quepa esta differencia de condiciones, como suele acaescer, ¿quién negará que aya contienda en cosa que de tantas maneras se entienda?" (80–81).

The *Tragicomedia*'s prologue also reveals that the *argumentos* to each act were written by the *Comedia*'s printers rather than by Fernando de Rojas, which means that these summaries represent still another distinct element of the final text. In addition, the *Tragicomedia* includes three concluding octaves written by Rojas, with verses that indicate that the work's lascivious quality should not distract the reader from its didactic nature and *honesta lavor* (344). Finally, the *Tragicomedia*'s Toledo edition of 1514 presents one additional act, now called the *Auto de Traso*, which was placed between the existing Acts XVIII and XIX.[3]

As a result of *Celestina*'s unusual textual development, the modern reader faces a number of different and often conflictive elements in the final work. First of all, there is the original *Auto*, which may have gone through different versions before reaching Fernando de Rojas's hands, and which may have been altered by Rojas himself before appearing as Act I of the *Comedia*. There are also the fifteen new acts of the *Comedia*, along with the printer's *argumentos* (1499); the opening letter and Alonso de Proaza's colophon (1500); the five additional acts of the *Tragicomedia*, the new prologue, and the author's closing verses (1500 or 1502); and finally the *Auto de Traso* (1514).

With this series of different texts already complicating the task of the modern reader, each addition to the work represents a further difficulty because these revisions often comment on or alter the existing sections of *Celestina*. Moreover, as a result of the work's erratic textual evolution and careless printing history, we are faced with an endless number of variants among the earliest editions of the *Comedia* and the *Tragicomedia*. Although *Celestina* is undoubtedly an extreme case, Bruce W. Wardropper has observed that many masterpieces of Spanish

---

3. Modern editions typically exclude the *Auto de Traso*; this act, however, is found at the end of the Marciales edition of *Celestina* (2:295–301).

Renaissance and Baroque literature are "decidedly undecidable text[s]" that are characterized by fundamental critical and philological uncertainties (1987, 179). Nevertheless, even though it is impossible to reconstruct definitive versions of long-lost manuscripts, Wardropper insists that philological hermeneutics are important for modern scholars, this critical approach being capable of solving many of the complexities of textual indeterminacy.

One of the best-known examples of the textual difficulties in *Celestina* occurs in the second scene of Act I, moments after Calisto awakens and calls out to his servant Sempronio. The *galán* asks the servant to open the room and make the bed, and once Sempronio follows his instructions Calisto tells him: "Cierra la ventana y dexa la tiniebla acompañar al triste y al desdichado la ceguedad. Mis pensamientos tristes no son dignos de luz. ¡O bienadventurada muerte aquella que deseada a los afligidos viene! ¡O si viniéssedes agora, Eras y Crato, médicos, sentiríades mi mal! ¡O piedad de silencio, inspira en el plebérico coraçón, por que sin esperança de salud no embíe el spíritu perdido con el desastrado Píramo y de la desastrada Tisbe!" (I, 88–89).

Shortly after the publication of the first editions of the *Comedia*, the *Tragicomedia* changes the names of the doctors Heras and Crato, as well as the allusion to the *piedad de silencio*.[4] The passage in the *Tragicomedia* reads: "¡O si viniéssedes agora, *Crato y Galieno*, médicos, sentiríades mi mal! ¡O piedad *celestial*, inspira en el plebérico coraçón . . . !" (I, 88). It appears that, no more than three years after the publication of the *Comedia*, there was already a minor *contienda* over the correct version of this paragraph. More important, the dispute about this passage still exists to this day, as noted in Dorothy Severin's edition of *Celestina*: "Otra indicación de la diversa autoría del primer acto se encuentra en esta frase problemática: 'Eras y Crato médicos . . . o piedad de silencio' que lee la *Comedia*. La lectura reconstruida debe referirse a Erasístrato, médico de Seleuco Nicator ('¡O piedad de Seleuco!'), que fue llamado para curar al hijo del rey, víctima de una locura de amor. Seleuco fue tenido como modelo de piedad al ceder su propia esposa a su hijo por encontrarse éste perdidamente enamorado de su madrastra" (88 n. 10).

---

4. Charles B. Faulhaber's transcription (1991) of the Biblioteca de Palacio Manuscript contains a shorter and much different version of this passage: "Saca la vela y dexa la tiniebla aconpañar al triste, y al desdichado la ceguedad. Mis tristes pensamientos no son dignos de luz. ¡O bienaventurada muerte aquella que, deseadja, alos aflitos viene!" (32). There is also a modification to this passage partially visible in the lower margin, but it is in a different handwriting and apparently represents a later change to the manuscript: "sentirías mi mal? ¡O piedad de Seleuco!" (32).

Severin respects the reference to *Crato y Galieno* found in the Zaragoza edition of the *Tragicomedia* (1507), and presents this correction to the text in the footnotes to Act I. Miguel Marciales, in his own edition of *Celestina*, proposes a similar version of this passage, again with a direct reference to Erasístrato. Nevertheless, Marciales places the reference directly within the text, because he considers it to be the most logical and acceptable version available. According to Marciales, the correct form of the passage is "Cierra la ventana y dexa la tiniebla acompañar al triste, y al desdichado la ceguedad. Mis pensamientos tristes no son dinos de luz. ¡O bienaventurada muerte aquella que, desseada, a los afligidos viene! ¡O! ¡si biviesses agora Erasístrato, médico, ¿sentiríades de mi mal? ¡O piedad seleucial!, inspira en el plebérico coraçón por que sin esperança de salud no embíe el espíritu perdido con el desastrado Píramo y la desdichada Tisbe!" (II, 19).

While other editors would agree with the changes that Marciales proposes, his justification for this variant would find far less critical support. Marciales studies the textual problems that appear in the first act, and he concludes that many of these difficulties can be resolved through a minor change in the interpretation of the primitive text. Marciales believes that the frequent misreadings of Act I

> son consecuencia del evidente problema que hay en la Cena 1ª del Auto I, cuya única solución es la que he propuesto y es la única lógica, sin violentar ni forzar el texto: en la concepción primera de Cota [según Marciales, el autor del *Auto*] Melibea era una mujer casada, una segunda Lucrecia de la *Historia de duobus amantibus*. Sin duda la concepción originaria del [*Auto*] es esta. Melibea es la esposa de un *Pléber* o *Pléberis* o *Plebero* y Calisto venía a ser un segundo Pánfilo o Eurialo. Así se explica la frase, *O pïedad seleucial (seleucal), inspira en el pléberico coraçón, porque sin esperança de salud no embíe el espíritu . . . a que se pierda por suicidio, tal como Píramo y Tisbe. . . .* La piedad de Seleuco debe inspirar en el corazón de Pleber(i)o para que este le ceda a Melibea. No hay otra interpretación posible. Rojas respetó en el Esbozo hasta este logogrífico pasaje, y se limitó a deducir mal del adjetivo *plebérico* un sustantivo *Pleberio*. (1:83–84)

P. E. Russell, like Marciales, places the references to Erasístrato directly within the first act, but in brackets to indicate the changes he makes to his base Burgos text of 1499: "¡O si [viviesses agora Erasístrato, médico, sentirías] mi mal! O piedad [seleucal], inspira en el plebérico coraçón, por que, sin esperança de salud, no embíe el espíritu perdido con el desastrado Píramo y la desdichada Tisbe!" (I, 214–15). While Russell clearly indicates that the reference to Erasístrato representa a modification of the original text, he seems as sure as Marciales of the correct form of the passage: "[N]o hay duda de que el pasaje incorpora una reminiscencia de una historieta de Valerio Máximo . . . donde se habla de la curación del médico Erasístrato (hacia 300 a.C.). 'Eras y Crato' debe resultar, pues, de una mala lección de 'Erasístrato' por un amanuense o cajista, con introducción de los verbos en plural para ajustarse a la duplicación de los nombres. El *viniéssedes* . . . es seguramente errata por *viviessedes*" (I, 215 n. 2).

The variants found in the different editions of *Celestina* represent a rather brusque transition in a passage that refers to the doctors Heras and Crato in the *Comedia*, that changes to Crato and Galieno in the *Tragicomedia*, and that modern editors now correct with the single name of Erasístrato. Nevertheless, despite the current popularity of this version of the *Auto*, the first scholar to propose this textual modificación was none other than Ramón Menéndez Pidal in his *Antología de prosistas castellanos* of 1917: "¡O si vinéssedes agora Erasístrato, médico, sentiríades mi mal! ¡O piedad de Seleuco . . . !" (69–70). According to Menéndez Pidal, it is logical to eliminate the references to Heras and Crato because there is no mention of the two doctors prior to the *Comedia*'s publication. For this reason, the *Tragicomedia*'s printers, or perhaps Fernando de Rojas himself, saw fit to correct this obvious error that somehow found its way into the *Comedia*: "Como no existen tales médicos Eras y Crato, otras ediciones trataron de corregir, y así hallamos 'Crato y Galieno' y 'piedad de Celeuco' (1514, 1595); 'Erasístrato y Galieno' y 'piedad de Seleuto'. . . (1570 y otras)" (69 n. 1).

Menéndez Pidal's reading of the passage is quite unexceptionable if we follow the basic assumptions behind the modification of the text: since we have no information to confirm the existence of Heras and Crato, then any reference to these fictional doctors must be a misreading on the part of Fernando de Rojas or the book's printers. Don Ramón therefore proposes adapting the variants from the *Tragicomedia* of 1570, which refers to *Erasístrato y Galieno* instead of *Eras y Crato* or *Crato y Galieno*: "Nuestra corrección la más sencilla: *eras & crato* es confusión facilísima por *erasistrato*, dado que la c y la t en la escritura medieval tiene forma muy semejante, y *silencio* por *sileuco* o *seleuco* también se confunden. . . . Esta corrección es también la única exacta: Calisto alude a una anécdota de *Valerio Máximo*" (69 n. 1).

Martín de Riquer (1957), the second scholar to write on the variants in this passage, also concludes that Rojas must have altered the original *Auto* because he did not understand the allusion to the classical doctor Erasístrato. Although Riquer agrees with the reconstruction first provided by Menéndez Pidal, he demonstrates one fundamental change in his interpretation of the passage. As noted above, Menéndez Pidal first proposes the corrected version of Erasístrato because he believes that the two doctors Heras and Crato did not exist in classical antiquity. Riquer, on the other hand, notes that these medical men were historical characters who appear in the work of Martial and Celsus:

> La verdadera lectura de este pasaje es, indiscutiblemente, la que adoptó Menéndez Pidal en los fragmentos de *La Celestina* que publicó en la *Antología de prosistas españoles* . . . [Rojas] evidentemente ignoraba la anécdota de Antíoco y Seleuco. . . . En las primeras ediciones (1499 y 1501) enmendó el nombre para él incomprensible (sin duda alguna por difícil lectura del manuscrito) en *Eras y Crato* porque sabía que existieron unos médicos de la antigüedad así llamados. En efecto, Marcial habla del primero . . . y Celso del segundo. (380–81)

With these observations, Riquer not only demonstrates a surprising familiarity with the conditions of the anonymous manuscript found by Fernando de Rojas centuries earlier, but more important, he uses completely contrary arguments to support the very same conclusion previously reached by Menéndez Pidal. As noted above, Don Ramón believed that it was necessary to suppress a reference to two doctors that never existed, but forty years later Riquer argues that Rojas altered the text precisely because he was familiar with these supposedly fictitious medical men.[5] Moreover, Riquer provides a long quote from Menéndez Pidal to buttress his own position, but he conveniently neglects to provide the key phrase from Don Ramón's 1917 edition of the *Antología de prosistas castellanos:* "Como no existen tales médicos Eras ni Crato" (69 n. 1).

Keith Whinnom (1977) studies the same passage from Act I and, much like Riquer, recognizes the existence of the doctors Heras and Crato. According to Whinnom, "Heras and Crato are the names of doctors mentioned by Martial and Celsus" (197). Moreover, following the lead of Menéndez Pidal and Riquer, the English scholar concludes that

---

5. Miguel Garci-Gómez (1982) observes: "Esta lectura del maestro [Menéndez Pidal] recibió incondicional apoyo en su discípulo Martín de Riquer, a pesar de que éste se muestra ya conocedor de la existencia de dos personajes, médicos, con los nombres de Eras y Crato" (11).

"this corrupt passage in the early editions of *Celestina* conceals an obvious reference to an anecdote in Valerius Maximus, in which the doctor Erasistratus persuades Seleucus, Satrap of Babylonia, that the cure for his son's malady is to give him the girl for whom he is pining" (197).

Despite the arguments presented by Menéndez Pidal, Riquer, Whinnom, Marciales, and Russell, the textual modification presented in a slim volume some eight decades ago is neither as simple nor as conclusive as these scholars believe. It is interesting to note that Menéndez Pidal affirms that his version of the text is "la única exacta" (69 n. 1). Riquer adds that this modification represents "la verdadera lectura," which he can attest to "indiscutiblemente" (380). Whinnom writes about the *Auto*'s "obvious reference" to Erasístrato (197), while Marciales believes—in typically understated fashion—that "[n]o hay otra interpretación posible" (I, 84). Finally, Russell indicates that "[n]o hay duda" about the correct reading of the passage (I, 215 n. 2). Severin's more subdued observation that the original passage "debe referirse a Erasístrato" seems rather refreshing in comparison (I, 88 n. 10).

In spite of the confident affirmations of several generations of Hispanists, María Rosa Lida de Malkiel notes that this textual modification is more complicated than it seems. She believes that it would be difficult for Rojas to change the verbs in the plural form that refer to Heras and Crato in the *Comedia* (*viniésssedes* and *sentiríades*), especially because "n[o] hay modificaciones semejantes entre los demás retoques del acto I" (18). Lida de Malkiel's observations are unsurprising, as even Whinnom notes that if the *Auto*'s reference to Erasístrato had been modified in favor of Heras and Crato, then this would mean that "in the space of two lines someone effected half a dozen repairs to the original manuscript" (197). Lida de Malkiel also rejects Rojas's supposed ignorance of the name Erasístrato because there is no "motivo para suponer que Rojas desconociese a Valerio Máximo, bastante difundido en Castilla en el siglo XV" (18). According to Lida, any modification in the passage would be caused by "deturpaciones ajenas" to the text, in which case the most probable explanation would be changes made by the book's printers.

Other modern scholars offer different alternatives to Menéndez Pidal's 1917 reading of the passage. Julio Cejador y Frauca's early edition of *Celestina* reads: "¡O si viniéssedes agora, Hipocrates e Galeno, médicos, ¿sentiríades mi mal? ¡O piedad de silencio, inspira en el Plebérico coraçon, porque sin esperança de salud no embíe el espíritu perdido con el desastrado Píramo e de la desdichada Tisbe!" (I, 35–36). According to Cejador, he alters the text of the existing versions of

Celestina because he believes that "[n]o hubo tales médicos Eras, Creato ni Erasistrato" (35, n. 13). While Cejador's modification seems arbitrary, Manuel Criado del Val's and G. D. Trotter's critical edition of *Celestina* uses the *Tragicomedia* rather than the *Comedia* as the base text for this passage: "¡O, si viniessedes agora, Crato y Galieno, médicos, sentiriades mi mal! ¡O piedad celestial!" (I, 24–25).

Miguel Garci-Gómez (1982) also rejects the change to Erasístrato proposed by Menéndez Pidal, precisely because we know that Heras and Crato were authentic historical figures that appear in classical literature. Garci-Gómez believes that the textual variants found throughout the sixteenth century suggest that Heras and Crato were not well known in Renaissance Spain, but the most important aspect of this article is the specific identification of the two doctors and the explanation of their appropriate place in the primitive text. According to Garci-Gómez, Martial's *Epigram* indicates that "Heras es el médico que trata a Phrige, quien a causa de mucho beber, estaba ciego de un ojo y legañoso del otro" (12). The medical studies of Cassius and Celsus also include mention of Heras's and Crato's prescriptions to cure hearing problems. The medical specialties of these doctors, the eye and the ear, are directly related to "la tiniebla" and "la ceguedad" that Calisto describes in this passage of Act I, as well as to "la piedad de silencio" that he requests a short time later (I, 88). As a result of Garci-Gómez's analysis of the historical figures of Heras and Crato, the *Comedia*'s original version of the passage makes perfect sense, and therefore does not require the extensive and often awkward modification that it has received throughout the centuries.

Although Garci-Gómez's identification of Heras and Crato appears to be a small detail in the reading of the first act, this passage takes on an additional significance if we consider the contemporary theories on erotic melancholy mentioned in the first two chapters of the present study.[6] As noted above, medieval and Renaissance writers believed that amorous passion leads to lovesickness or *amor hereos*, an illness that

---

6. Michael Solomon (1997) concludes that the reference to Erasístrato "would also draw a physician's attention towards a diagnosis of *amor hereos*" (197 n. 21). Donald McGrady, who favors the reading of Heras and Crato, concludes: "Garci-Gómez greatly overstates his case when he suggests (12) that both doctors were well known, and that their recipes (as registered by Celsus) are appropriate for Calisto" (18 n. 25). In fact, Garci-Gómez clearly indicates that the two were *not* well known: "Hay que admitir que Eras y Crato no debieron ser personajes fácilmente reconocibles. El mismo autor sintió la necesidad de aclarar su profesión de *médicos*, menos necesario de haberse tratado de personajes más célebres" (1982, 11). Moreover, this chapter demonstrates that the medical expertise of Heras and Crato is exactly appropriate for Calisto's ailment.

produces "paleness, sleeplessness, groaning, sighing, loss of appetite, palpitation of the heart, and even death" (Martin 11–12). Although the symptoms of *amor hereos* are well known to modern scholars, it is important to note that the sight and hearing are the two essential vehicles for the spread of the disease in both the Arabic and European medical traditions. According to the *Hayât al-Hayawân*, written by the fourteenth-century scholar Ad-Damîris, "Abd-ar Rahmân b. Nasr states that physicians hold *ardent and excessive love (al-'ishk)* to be a disease arising from sight and hearing. . . . It is of several degrees and has several stages following one another, the first . . . is called *approval* which arises from sight and hearing; this stage gains in strength by remembering for a long time the good points and beautiful qualities of the object of love, and then becomes *affection*" (qtd. in Lowes 516–17).

As Mary Frances Wack has noted, the concept of *al-'ishk* was brought to Europe in the late eleventh century by the monk Constantine the African, who coined the Latin name *amor hereos* to describe the malady (32–38). Constantine's *Viaticum* became a standard reference work in Europe for centuries, and his ideas enjoyed wide distribution through the glosses and commentaries of Gerard of Berry, Peter of Spain, and Bona Fortuna. For this reason, the causes and symptoms of *al-'ishk* in the scientific tract above are almost identical to the characteristics of *amor hereos* that appear in European studies from the Middle Ages to the Baroque period.[7]

Andreas Capellanus writes in the *De amore* that a blind man cannot fall in love because he cannot establish the initial visual contact with a woman, although a person who goes blind after falling in love maintains the image of his beloved in his memory (35). Daniel Sennert, author of the seventeenth-century *Practical Physick*, writes that lovesickness occurs when the woman's impression is "received by the sight or discourse [and is] strongly imprinted upon the memory" (qtd. in Soufas 1990, 67). Robert Burton in *The Anatomy of Melancholy* also emphasizes the visual and auditory nature of heroical love. According

---

7. See Wack for a discussion of Constantine and his commentators, as well as for a selection from the actual Latin texts. For an analysis of how Arabic medical texts influenced the European notion of lovesickness and amorous literature, see McVaugh 14–15; Klibansky, Panovsky, and Saxl 82–97; García Ballester; and Jacquart. The relationship between *al-'ishk* and *amor hereos* was recognized throughout the centuries. For example, Andreas Laurentius writes in the English translation of *A Discourse of the Preservation of the Sight* (1599): "There is another kind of melancholic verie ordinary and common, which the Greeke Phisitions call *Erotike*, because it commeth of a furie and raging loue; the Arabians call it *Iliscus*, and the common sort, the diuine Passion" (117).

to Burton, the first contact between two lovers occurs through the medium of the eyes, but this initial attraction grows stronger if they live near each other or if they have the opportunity to converse or trade letters. These amorous allurements are particularly effective in the evening hours, and they become even more powerful if the woman has a sweet voice or if she plays a musical instrument (3:150).

One of the most influential medieval studies of *amor hereos* appears in a section of the *Lilio de Medicina*, written by the French scholar Bernardus Gordonius (c. 1258–1318). The 1495 Spanish translation explains the causes and symptoms of the disease and confirms the importance of the eyes in the development of the illness: "Amor que 'hereos' se dize es solicitud melancólica por causa de amor de mugeres. . . . E tanto está corrompido el iuyzio & la razón que continua mente piensa en ella: & dexa todas sus obras: en tal manera que sy alguno fabla conel non lo entiende: por que es en continuo pensamiento: esta 'solicitud melancólica' se llama. . . . [Las] Señales Son que pierden el sueño & el comer & el beuer & se enmagresce todo su cuerpo: saluo los ojos" (qtd. in Seniff 14–15).

According to Ioan P. Couliano (1987), Gordonius believes that for a man in love, vision is not affected during *amor hereos*, because the image of the woman penetrates the man's body and spirit through the eyes. The image of the woman is converted into a phantasm that invades and controls the lover's brain and prevents his full use of reason. Despite their central function in the development of lovesickness, Couliano indicates that the eyes are not affected by the *inamorato*'s mental and physical decay, because the illness obliges the lover to reclaim visual contact with his beloved: "If the eyes do not partake of the organism's general decay, it is because the spirit uses those corporeal apertures to reestablish contact with the object that was converted into the obsessing phantasm: the woman" (21).[8]

Since the rest of the body suffers a noticeable decay during love melancholy, the *inamorato*'s eyes take on an unmistakable physical appearance that reveals his illness. This symptom of *amor hereos* was first analyzed by John Livingston Lowes in a seminal article of 1913. Lowes studies the significance of a passage of *The Knight's Tale*—one

---

8. This uncontrollable desire to observe the beloved comes from the *Phaedrus*, in which Plato explains that although love affects the *inamorato*'s soul, this spiritual passion ceases when the lover reestablishes visual contact with the beloved (251b–252a; 108). Although the necessity of seeing the *amada* is also found in Castiglione's *Il libro del cortegiano* (LXV–LXVI) and in Marsilio Ficino's *De amore* (see Chapter 1, n. 6 above), Lawrence Babb notes that other sixteenth-century writers accepted similar Platonic ideas (132 n. 33).

of the best-known sections of *The Canterbury Tales*—that describes the physical and mental state of Arcite after his return to Thebes. Although the knight is no longer a prisoner in Athens, he has lost visual contact with his beloved Emelye, and this absence leaves him sick and overcome with erotic melancholy:

> His slep, his mete, his drynke, is him byraft,
> That lene he wex and drye as is a shaft;
> His eyen holwe, and grisly to biholde,
> His hewe falow and pale as asshen colde. (1361-64)

According to Lowes, one of the first allusions to the lover's hollow and sunken eyes is found in a medical tract by Oribasius (325-403): "Subsecuntur autem quidem amorem languint, quorum sunt haec signa: oculi sunt concavi et non lacrimatur" (qtd. in Lowes 519). Rhazes (860-930)—possibly the best-known Arabic doctor after Avicenna—also indicates that among the many symptoms of *amor hereos* are the "visus debilis: *et* oculi sicci *et* concaui: *et non* lachrymantur" (qtd. in Lowes 508). Doctor Abulcasim (tenth century) also studies the disease and indicates: "Signa dilectionis sunt, q*uoniam* oculi sunt concaui. . . . Color vero faciei est citrinus & omnia sua membra sunt sicca" (qtd. in Lowes 511). Avicenna (980-1037) confirms these characteristics of the disease in his *Canon*, which served as a basic medical text in Europe until the seventeenth century: "The signs [of lovesickness] are hollowness and dryness of the eyes, with no moisture except when crying, continuous blinking of the eyelids, smiling as though he had seen something quite delightful or heard something agreeable . . . and he is either joyful and smiling, or despondent and in tears, murmuring of love; and specially when remembering his absent loved one; and all the bodily parts are dried up, except the eyes which are swollen due to much crying and wakefulness" (qtd. in Jackson 355).

There are many other medieval and Renaissance texts that corroborate these symptoms of erotic melancholy. Constantine the African writes in the *Viaticum* (late eleventh century) that "[s]ince this illness has more serious consequences for the soul, that is, excessive thoughts, their eyes always become hollow [and] move quickly because of the soul's thoughts [and] worries to find and possess what they desire" (qtd. in Wack 189). Gerard of Berry adds in his gloss of Constantine's *Viaticum* (1236 or 1237) that the symptoms of the malady include "sunken eyes, since they follow the *spiritus* racing to the place of the estimative [faculty]; also, dryness of the eyes and lack of tears unless weeping occurs on account of the desired object" (qtd. in

Wack 201). According to the great Catalan doctor Arnaldus de Vilanova (c. 1240–1311), among the "signa distinctiua hereos" are "siccitas *et* profunditas oculorum" (qtd. in Lowes 496 n. 3). Daniel Sennert (1572–1637) adds in the English translation of *The Practical Physick:* "This dilirium from Love may be referred to as the Melancholy before mentioned. . . . The face is pale . . . they are watchful, their body pines, their eyes are hollow and heavy for want of Spirits" (qtd. in Jackson 358). According to the Dutch doctor Peter van Foreest (1522–97), "These are the signs of . . . [love] madness: The eyes are hollow, dry, tearless and blinking" (qtd. in Jackson 364). In *Erotomania*, the masterful study by Jacques Ferrand (1612; English translation 1640), the lover's eyes are "hollow, and sunke into their head, dry, and without teares; yet alwaies twinkling with a kind of smiling looke" (125).

If we understand the causes and symptoms of lovesickness in Renaissance Europe, then we can see the importance of the reference to Heras and Crato in the second scene of Act I. According to the principal authorities on love melancholy in western Europe, the eyes and the ears are not only the instruments that cause the initial effects of the disease, but more important, the eyes reflect one of its most obvious physical symptoms. For this reason, doctors familiar with the illnesses of sight and hearing—such as the two distinguished medical authorities Heras and Crato—would correctly diagnose Calisto's lovesick condition.

Moreover, the visual and auditory basis of *amor hereos* is not limited to scientific and philosophical treatises; this aspect of the malady appears in amorous literature throughout the centuries. Dante, for example, writes in *La vita nuova* that he fell in love with Beatrice at the age of nine when "a li miei occhi apparve prima la gloriosa donna de la mia mente" (46) ("to my eyes first appeared the glorious lady of my mind" [47]). The image of this beautiful young woman accompanies Dante constantly during the following nine years, until she finally grants the poet her benevolent gaze during a second chance encounter: "[E] passando per una via, volse li occhi verso quella parte ov'io era molto pauroso, e per la sua ineffabile cortesia . . . mi salutoe molto virtuosamente, tanto che me parve allora vedere tutti li termini de la beatitudine" (48) ("[A]nd passing along a street, she turned her eyes to that place where I stood in great fear, and in her ineffable courtesy . . . she greeted me with exceeding virtue, such that I then seemed to see all the terms of beatitude" [49]). After this meeting, Dante begins to suffer the dreams and visions of *amor hereos*, and he spends much of his time in bed dreaming about his beloved Beatrice.

Joanot Martorell's *Tirant lo Blanc* demonstrates the same process of visual lovesickness the moment that the knight meets Princess Carmesina in the emperor of Constantinople's palace. While Tirant's ears listen to the emperor's words in the royal chamber, his eyes are smitten when he sees the young woman's beautiful figure:

> Dient l'Emperador tals o semblants paraules les orelles de Tirant estaven atentes a les raons, e los ulls d'altra part contemplaven la gran bellea de Carmesina. E per la gran calor que feia . . . estava mig descordada mostrant en los pits dues pomes de paradís que crestallines parien, les quales donaren entrada als ulls de Tirant, que a'allí avant no trobaren la porta per on eixir, e tostemps foren apresonats en poder de persona lliberta. (374)
>
> (As Tirant listened to the emperor's words, his eyes were fixed upon the fair princess. It had been so hot . . . that she had half-unbuttoned her blouse and he could see her breasts, which were like two heavenly crystalline apples. They allowed Tirant's gaze to enter but not to depart, and he remained in her power till the end of his days. [189])

Although Carmesina's striking beauty leaves Tirant obsessed with her paradisiacal *pomes* and unsure of the precise location of the *porta*, the physical aspect of his love affects him in much the same way as Dante's spiritual love for Beatrice. After leaving the emperor's chambers, Tirant returns to his room to lie down, but because of his mental condition he is unsure of which part of the bed he is lying on: "Tirant pres llicència de tots e anáse'n a la posada, entràse'n en una cambra e posà lo cap sobre un coisi als peus del llit" (CXVIII, 374) ("Tirant took his leave of them and returned to his chamber, where he lay [his head upon a cushion at the foot of the bed]" [190]).

These characteristics of lovesickness explain much of Calisto's unusual behavior in the second scene of Act I. At the beginning of the scene, Calisto asks Sempronio to make the bed so that the *galán* can go to his room and lie down, much like Dante or Tirant would have done. The *galán* then asks Sempronio to close the window so that he can reproduce the state of darkness and blindness that reflects his inner turmoil: "Cierra la ventana y dexa la tiniebla acompañar al triste y al desdichado la ceguedad. Mis pensamientos tristes no son dinos de luz" (I, 88).[9] Although this blindness would have prevented Calisto's

---

9. Teresa S. Soufas notes that melancholics often seek out darkness, an external state that is related to the internal condition of the black bile that supposedly causes melan-

lovesickness in the first place, this solution comes too late for the young man because the image of his beloved has already overwhelmed his mind and spirit. Calisto is now dominated by his "pensamientos tristes" (I, 88), a state that recalls the continuous contemplation and mental agitation described by many specialists on the subject of *amor hereos*. After suffering these sad thoughts, the *galán* desperately needs the "piedad de silencio" (I, 88) to forget the cruel words that he has heard from Melibea's phantasm in the *Auto*'s first scene.

Because of Calisto's miserable mental and physical state at the start of *Celestina*, it is natural that such doctors of sight and hearing as Heras and Crato would recognize the young man's obvious lovesick symptoms and would understand the extent of his illness. More important, Fernando de Rojas—who undoubtedly knew the principal characteristics of amorous literature in contemporary Europe—is also aware of the way that Calisto must have fallen in love. For this reason, when Rojas provides an explanation of Calisto's overwhelming ardor, he relates the *galán*'s condition directly to the senses of sight and hearing. As Pármeno tells his master at the beginning of Act II, "Señor, porque perderse el otro día el neblí fue causa de tu entrada en la huerta de Melibea a le buscar; la entrada causa de la veer y hablar, la habla engendró amor; el amor parió tu pena; la pena causará perder tu cuerpo y el alma y hazienda" (II, 134–35). According to Rojas, Calisto's heroical love began when he had the opportunity to *veer y hablar* with Melibea, and in turn *la habla* led directly to his amorous condition. This visual and auditive contact not only produces his subsequent *pena*, but also the other dreadful symptoms of *amor hereos*.

As noted by Wardropper, despite the inherent instability of Golden Age literature, a philological analysis of these texts is necessary to elucidate their original meaning and to demonstrate their underlying cultural referentiality. On the basis of this kind of study, we can conclude that the earliest reference to Heras and Crato in the first act of the *Comedia de Calisto y Melibea* was changed a number of times in the sixteenth century because the book's editors did not realize that these characters were doctors of sight and hearing, and that they had a very logical reason for appearing in this passage. In spite of the textual confusion that exists to this day, Garci-Gómez's astute observations about

---

choly (1987, 182). Rojas's continuation of *Celestina* emphasizes this quality in Calisto, as noted in Sempronio's words to the *galán* at the beginning of the second act: "[E]n viéndote solo, dizes desvaríos de hombre sin seso, sospirando, gemiendo, maltrobando, holgando con lo oscuro, desseando soledad, buscando nuevos modos de pensativo tormento" (II, 132).

the medical specialties of Heras and Crato suggest an important change in the editorial standards for the first act of *Celestina*. If we consider that Act I is an independent work of an unknown author or authors, then it is clear that we should use the oldest complete version of the *Auto* as the base text, which at this time is still the *Comedia* of 1499.[10] Any subsequent revisions to the first act merely add further instability to the final version of the primitive text, which means that it is preferable to reject later changes or modifications to Act I of *Celestina*, irrespective of whether they be the work of Fernando de Rojas, the work's printers, or modern editors and scholars.

---

10. Russell uses the 1499 *Comedia* as the base text, although he incorporates later modifications to Act I. McGrady, who believes that Heras and Crato were deliberate changes by Rojas, writes: "The lesson learned from this particular passage has to be applied to the entire work: editors must show more respect for the text of the *Comedia* of Burgos 1499, which in all likelihood is the princeps. Careful examinations of other presumed errors in the 1499 text will doubtless show that they too were perfectly normal usages at the time" (16).

4

Burton's *The Anatomy of Melancholy*

A Seventeenth-Century View of *Celestina*

Almost three decades ago, Otis H. Green noted that Calisto's irrational behavior in *Celestina* was symptomatic of the illness of love melancholy or *amor hereos*, the medieval disease whose most common symptoms include bouts of depression, sighing, and moaning, as well as insomnia and a loss of appetite. Although critics such as June Hall Martin, Michael Solomon, and I (1993a) have since studied the causes and effects of Calisto's lovesickness, only Frederick A. de Armas has noted the *galán*'s presence in Robert Burton's (1577–1640) *The Anatomy of Melancholy*, without question the most extensive early analysis of this illness written in English.[1] In this chapter I continue the research begun by de Armas, and analyze Calisto's as well as Celestina's role in *The Anatomy* in order to determine how Rojas's work was viewed by an English authority on the subject of love melancholy.[2] At the same

---

1. See also the parallel research by Anthony J. Cárdenas (1988) on love melancholy in the *Corbacho* and *Celestina*, as well as Michael Solomon's work on the *Corbacho* and the *Spill* (1997).
2. According to Michael Solomon, "F. A. de Armas and Anthony Cárdenas identify Calisto's ailment as 'love melancholy,' rather than the more medically precise *amor*

time, I consider whether Burton's seventeenth-century view of *Celestina* could be helpful to modern scholars of Spanish Renaissance literature.

The first edition of *The Anatomy* appeared in 1621, but Burton continued to review and expand the work over five more editions written during the next two decades.[3] Burton knew of *Cælestina* from the 1624 Latin translation titled the *Pornoboscodidascalus latinus* (School of Brothel Keeping), so the references to Rojas's work were evidently added to later editions of *The Anatomy*. The many citations and paraphrases in Burton's work suggest that he read virtually everything ever published on the subject of melancholy, and the addition of works such as *Celestina* to later editions of *The Anatomy* indicates that the subject of melancholy must have been a lifelong passion for the English writer.

It is remarkable to note that on a typical page, Burton quotes or summarizes passages from such diverse sources as the Bible, classical mythology, Aristotle, Petrarca, Seneca, Catullus, Saint Jerome, Bernardus

---

hereos. Their terminology, however, relies too heavily on primary sources from the sixteenth and seventeenth-century [sic] (Burton's *Anatomy*, 1621) and secondary sources. . . . Melancholy in antiquity and in the Middle Ages was less a diagnosis than a humor (black bile), and a humoral condition, or state of temperament. It is true that men identified as having melancholic compositions were more likely to develop certain diseases—including *amor hereos*—than others, but this is not the same as actually having a disease" (1989, 59 n. 6).

In reality, *amor hereos*, heroic love, love melancholy, erotique melancholy, *ferinus insanus amor*, erotomania, *erotes, mal de amores*, the Arabic *al-'ishk*, and women's *furor uterinus* were used throughout the centuries to describe the symptoms and the effects of the same illness. For example, the 1495 Spanish translation of the *Lilio de Medicina* indicates: "Amor que 'hereos' se dize es solicitud melancólica por causa de amor de mugeres . . . E tanto está corrompido el iuyzio & la razón que continuamente piensa en ella . . . por que es en continuo pensamiento: esta 'solicitud melancólica' se llama. . . . Verdadera mente esta pasion [de amor] es vna especia de melancolia" (qtd. in Seniff 14, 16).

Moreover, as Giorgio Agamben has noted, "[T]he nexus between love and melancholy . . . found its theoretical foundation in a medical tradition that constantly considered love and melancholy as related, if not identical, maladies. In this tradition, fully articulated in the *Viaticum* of the Arab physician Haly Abbas (who, through the tradition of Constantine the African, profoundly influenced medieval European medicine), love, which appeared with the name *amor hereos* or *amor heroycus*, and melancholy were catalogued in contiguous rubrics among the mental diseases [e.g., as in Arnaldo de Vilanova]. On occasion, as in the *Speculum doctrinale* of Vincent de Beauvais, they appeared in fact under the same rubric: 'de melancolia nigra et canina et de amore qui ereos dicitur'" (16–17).

3. There are subsequent editions of 1624, 1628, 1632, 1638, and a final, posthumous edition of 1651. The last edition, finished shortly before Burton's death in 1640, is approximately 60 percent longer than the original (Babb 15).

Gordonius, Chaucer, and Giovanni Michelle Savonarola. These varied references include short passages of fictional and nonfictional work, varied opinions, lines of poetry, direct quotations, and extensive paraphrases, all thrown together in a style that is both learned and whimsical. This intertextuality is so extensive that approximately one-third of the work consists of direct citations, another third of paraphrasing, and the remaining one-third of Burton's original discourse (Vicari 3).

The varied nature of this *cento* notwithstanding, the purpose of Burton's unique writing style is not to collect a mass of material freely appropriated from other writers. Instead, Burton takes great care to identify his hundreds of sources, a technique that reveals the extent of his scholarly research as well as the depth of his knowledge on the subject of love melancholy: "As a good housewife out of divers fleeces weaves one piece of cloth . . . I have laboriously collected this cento out of divers writers, and that *sine injuria*, I have wronged no authors, but given every man his own . . . I cite and quote mine authors . . . *sumpsi, non surripui* [I have taken, not filched] . . . I can say of myself, Whom have I injured? The matter is theirs most part, and yet mine, *apparet unde sumptum sit* [it is plain when it was taken] . . . the composition and method is ours only, and shows a scholar" (1:24–25).

Burton is as much a scribe and an intellectual as he is a writer, and the extent of his research and knowledge is truly exceptional. For example, even though he owned only one Spanish book and apparently did not know the language well (O'Connell 16), he cites the American writings of Bartolomé de las Casas, Father José de Acosta, Christopher Columbus, and Hernán Cortés. In Spanish literature he mentions not only *Celestina*, but also *Don Quixote, Guzmán de Alfarache, Amadís de Gaula,* and *Palmerín de Oliva*. In addition, he refers to the Latin medical studies of Nicolás Monardes, Luis Mercado, and Francisco Valles, along with the religious and philosophical writings of Juan Luis de la Cerda, Arnaldus de Vilanova, Pedro de Morales, Bernardino Gómez-Miedes, Martín Azpilcueta, Domingo de Soto, San Francisco Xavier, and Luis Vives. Nevertheless, despite the extensive presence of Hispanic letters throughout the pages of *The Anatomy*, it is important to remember that these Spanish works represent but a small part of the approximately 1,250 authors that appear in the final edition of the work (O'Connell 59), as the diversity of this *cento* sweeps across much of the western canon from the Greek and Roman world all the way up to the Baroque period.

According to Burton, melancholy is a "universal . . . madness, an epidemical disease" (1:121) that includes such vexing personal problems as dementia, anger, hypochondria, and depression. Quoting the

Hispano-Roman writer and philosopher Seneca, Burton writes: "[L]ove is madness, a hell, an incurable disease; *impotentem et insanam libidinem* Seneca calls it, an impotent and raging lust" (1:114). In fact, the illness is so widespread in contemporary Europe that Burton himself admits to suffering from the effects of melancholia. *The Anatomy* thus serves not only as a study of the causes and cures of this terrible malady, but also as a means of alleviating Burton's own ailment through his writing and research: "I write of melancholy, by being busy to avoid melancholy. There is no greater cause of melancholy than idleness, 'no better cure than business,' as Rhasis holds" (1:20).

While the composition of *The Anatomy* helps to ease Burton's personal suffering, the principal goal of the work is didactic in nature. He anatomizes this horrible disease—or analyzes it in minute detail—so that others will gain greater knowledge about the illness and learn to defend themselves from its worst symptoms and effects. Or, to put it in a way that would be more familiar to Fernando de Rojas, Burton seeks to provide the reader of *The Anatomy* with the *defensivas armas* that will guard against this illness: "[M]y purpose and endeavor is, in the following discourse to anatomize this humour of melancholy, through all his parts and species, as it is an habit, or an ordinary disease, and that philosophically, medicinally, to show the causes, symptoms, and several cures of it, that it may be the better avoided" (1:120).

Although Burton analyzes many different kinds of melancholy in *The Anatomy*, the most important section for Fernando de Rojas's readers is the Third Partition, titled "Love Melancholy," which contains eight of the work's nine references to the *Tragicomedia*. According to Burton, there are three different kinds of love melancholy: heroical love, which is the ailment that affects Calisto and other lovesick young men; jealousy, which in many ways is a more serious illness than *amor hereos*; and religious melancholy. The symptoms of Calisto's love melancholy are anticipated in *The Anatomy*'s frontispiece and opening poem, both of which refer to the most common characteristics of the young European *inamorato*.

The frontispiece contains ten scenes, with an engraving of the author surrounded by the images of a madman, a hypochondriac, a jealous man, and a superstitious man who is pictured as a praying Catholic monk. There is also a well-dressed young man surrounded by books, a lute, and sheet music, who is described in the opening poem as follows:

> I' th' under column there doth stand
> *Inamorato* with folded hand;
> Down hangs his head, terse and polite,

Some ditty sure he doth indite.
His lute and books about him lie,
As symptoms of his vanity. (1:7–8)

The description of the lovesick young man's poetic and musical creations recalls the numerous scenes where Calisto begins to *trovar* about his undying love for Melibea. As María Rosa Lida de Malkiel (1962) has observed, "El amor de Calisto está empapado de literatura" (333), and this form of amorous expression manifests itself through Calisto's original poetic creations as well as through his appropriation of traditional oral and written literature. In Act I, for example, Calisto asks his servant Sempronio to bring the lute into the bedroom, and he then begins to sing the absurd ditty, "¿Quál dolor puede ser tal, / que se yguale con mi mal?" (I, 91). While Sempronio quickly responds with the sarcastic comment that "Destemplado está este laúd" (I, 91), by the next morning Calisto is singing much better verse from the *cancionero* (VIII, 218).[4] Moreover, on his last morning of life he improves his lyrical expression to such an extent that he effortlessly recites *pie quebrado* verse about his beloved Melibea (XIII, 276).

In Burton's world, a young man affected by heroical love establishes a form of dialogical *vaivén* between his love life on the one hand and the traditions of amorous literature on the other. As Ruth A. Fox (1976) has observed in her study of *The Anatomy*, Burton believes that "as fictions make men love, men in love make fictions" (156). Poets have traditionally used love as the principal inspiration for their lyrical work; Burton indicates that ordinary lovers follow this same process but in reverse, as they employ lyrical poetry as a vehicle to express their amorous condition: "Amongst other good qualities an amorous fellow is endowed with, he must learn to sing and dance, play upon some instrument or other, as without all doubt he will, if he be truly touched with this loadstone of love. For as Erasmus had it . . . love will make them musicians, and compose ditties, madrigals, elegies, love-sonnets, and sing to several pretty tunes" (3:177).

Since Calisto exhibits many of the common characteristics of the *inamorato*, *The Anatomy*'s four references to the *galán*—along with

---

4. While Rojas gradually improves Calisto's poetic creations, he is conscious of the poor quality of the young man's first verses. As Sempronio notes in Act II, when Calisto is alone "[él] diz[e] desvaríos de hombre sin seso, sospirando, gemiendo, maltrobando" (II, 132). See Kassier for the importance of *cancionero* poetry in *Celestina*. I also note (1995) that the *galanes* in the Celestinesque genre often play the lute and sing *romances* as part of their lovesick condition.

one additional reference to the *fanfarrón* Centurio—appear in the member of the Third Partition titled "Symptoms or signs of Love-Melancholy, in Body, Mind, good, bad, & c." Burton writes that honest love is found only in the sacred institution of marriage, which he believes to be an "honourable, ... blessed calling" that "breeds true peace, tranquillity, content, and happiness" (3:52). While Burton indicates that nothing compares with the affectionate goodwill of conjugal love, the illness of heroical love—or *ferinus insanus amor* (3:56)—is so strong that it frequently manifests itself outside of marriage through a series of physical and mental symptoms.

Burton notes that the common signs of heroical love include "paleness, leanness, dryness ... [and] hollow ... eyes," and that the normal behavior consists of "cares, sighs, ... groans, griefs, sadness, want of appetite, & c." (3:133). These symptoms represent the normal manifestations of love melancholy found throughout the Middle Ages, but Burton believes that the extensive outward evidence of the illness is far less complex than its hidden, mental symptoms: "[T]he symptoms of the mind in Lovers are almost infinite, and so diverse, that no art can comprehend them; though they be merry sometimes, and rapt beyond themselves for joy, yet most part love is a plague, a torture, a hell, a bitter-sweet passion at last.... For in a word, the Spanish inquisition is not comparable to it" (1:141).

The *inamorato*'s existence is characterized by continual fits of agony and suffering; Burton writes, however, that these feelings can be temporarily alleviated by the lover's *lucida intervalla* or by his beloved's smile, pleasant look, or kiss. This change in the lover's behavior when he is favored by his *amada* is derived from the *Phaedrus*, in which Plato indicates that love is powerful enough to affect the *inamorato*'s soul, but that this spiritual passion is ameliorated when the lover reestablishes visual contact with his beloved (251b–252a; 108).[5] Unfortunately, while these brief moments of amorous ecstacy offer a momentary respite from the lover's suffering, they lead to another form of uncontrolled behavior. According to Burton, during these happy moments the lover is "too confident and rapt beyond himself, as if he had heard the nightingale in the spring before the cuckoo, or as Callisto was at Meliboea's presence, *Quis unquam hac mortali vita tam gloriosum corpus vidit? humanitatem transcendere videor*, etc. Who ever saw so glorious a sight, what man ever enjoyed such delight?" (¿Quién vido en esta vida cuerpo glorificado de ningún hombre como agora el mío? [I, 86]) (3:144).

5. See also Chapter 3, n. 8.

Although Calisto sinks into a lovesick depression at the end of *Celestina*'s first scene, his mystical rapture in Melibea's imaginary presence is caused by the same amorous melancholy that he exhibits throughout the work. Burton indicates that if the lover is favored by his *amada*, "There is no happiness in the world comparable to his, no content, no joy to this, no life to love, he is in paradise" (3:144). Even though Burton writes that the young lover alternates between moments of unbounded delight and periods of intolerable suffering, it is important to note that he experiences the continuous contemplation of his beloved irrespective of his specific psychological state. Burton believes that whether it appears in the evening or during the day, in the lover's waking hours or in his dreams, when he is joyful or depressed, the image of the *amada* is ever present in the lover's consciousness, as demonstrated by Calisto's behavior in Act I of *Celestina:*

> Howsoever his present state be pleasing or displeasing, 'tis continuate so long as he loves . . . desire hath no rest, she is his cynosure, *Hesperus et Vesper*, his morning and evening star . . . dreaming, waking, she is always in his mouth. . . . [S]he is the sole object of his senses, the substance of his soul . . . he magnifies her above measure, *totus in illa*, full of her, can breathe nothing but her. "I adore Meliboea," saith lovesick Callisto, "I believe in Meliboea, I honour, admire and love my Meliboea" ["Melibeo só, y a Melibea adoro, y en Melibea creo, y a Melibea amo" (I, 93)]. (3:146)

Since Calisto and other *inamorati* continually experience the mental image of their beloved, Burton believes that they can "think and dream of nought else" but her (3:147). This mental presence becomes even more pronounced during the evening than it is during the day (3:147), and on occasion her physical characteristics and behavior—"her sweet face, eyes, actions, gestures"—are so carefully measured by "that astrolabe of phantasy, and . . . so violently sometimes, with such earnestness and eagerness . . . so strong an imagination, that at length he thinks he sees her indeed; he talks with her, he embraceth her, Ixion-like . . . I see and meditate of naught but Leucippe" (3:148).

Because of the persistent, irrepressible power of the *inamorato*'s love melancholy, Burton writes, the young man constantly finds himself burning with passion for his *amada*. His suffering is such that even the fires of the greatest natural disasters pale in comparison to the strength of his ardor, as demonstrated by Calisto's overwhelming devotion for his beloved Melibea:

As Ætna rageth, so doth love, and more than Ætna or any material fire. . . . Vulcan's flames are but smoke to this. For fire, saith Xenophon, burns them alone that stand near it, or touch it; but this fire of love burneth and scorcheth afar off, and is more hot and vehement than any material fire. . . . For when Nero burnt Rome, as Callisto urgeth, he fired houses, consumed men's bodies and goods; but this fire devours the soul itself, "and one soul is worth an hundred thousand bodies." ["(M)ayor es la llama que dura ochenta años que la que en un día passa, y mayor la que mata un ánima que la que quemó cient mil cuerpos" (I, 92).] (3:149)

In Burton's melancholic world, love is an all-powerful force that causes scholars to ignore their studies and obliges rich men to squander their wealth. Men in love will resort to any form of treachery to fulfill their insane desires, being completely blinded by their emotions and thus incapable of wisdom or discretion. In fact, Burton writes, no matter how ugly or unpleasant the woman may be, the *inamorato* will always prefer his beloved to all of the ladies of the court, and even "before all the gods and goddesses themselves" (3:159). With this kind of exaggerated passion, the *inamorato* often attempts the most irrational and dangerous adventures, all in the name of his beloved. And, as occurs with Calisto, the lover's amorous condition can become so harmful that it leads him directly to his death and destruction: "'What shall I say,' saith Hædus, 'of their great dangers they undergo, single combats they undertake, how they will venture their lives, creep in at windows, gutters, climb over walls to come to their sweethearts . . . and if they be surprised, leap out at windows, cast themselves headlong down, bruising or breaking their legs or arms, and sometimes losing life itself,' as Callisto did for his lovely Meliboea" (3:162–63).

In addition to the perils that lovers endure because of their overwhelming passion, love melancholy also causes these foolish young men to fight and quarrel merely to impress their beloved. A typical example of these violent tendencies is "that Centurion in the Spanish *Cælestina*, [who] will kill ten men for his mistress Areusa, for a word of her mouth, he will cut bucklers in two like pippins, and flap down men like flies, *Elige quo mortis genere illum occidi cupis* (choose by what method you wish him killed)" (3:163) ("Hermana mía, mándame tú matar con diez hombres por tu servicio y no que ande una legua de camino a pie" [XV, 294]; "Allí te mostraré un repertorio en que ay sietecientas y setenta species de muertes; verás quál más te agradare" [XVIII, 316]). Although Burton cites many other examples of how far the *inamorati* will go to impress their *amadas*, he obviously does not realize that Centurio's words to the *mochachas* are pure braggadocio, and that in reality there is little to fear from the *fanfarrón*'s outlandish claims.

It is interesting to note that in Burton's explanation of the causes of heroical love, Calisto's melancholic ailment would appear to be a natural consequence not only of his personal background, but also of his national origin. Burton—like many other scholars who have written on the subject of love melancholy—believes that wealthy young men are the most likely to suffer from these intense passions.[6] This characteristic of erotic melancholy means that the aristocratic Calisto would be especially susceptible to this exaggerated and overwhelming ardor: "[I]f they be young, fortunate, rich, high-fed, and idle withal, it is almost impossible that they should live honest, not rage, and precipitate themselves into these inconveniences of burning lust" (3:62).

The air and climate found in warmer European countries also exacerbate the feverish passions of erotic melancholy, and as a result Burton concludes that the malady is particularly common in Spain and in other Mediterranean nations: "Your hot and Southern countries are prone to lust, and far more incontinent than those that live in the North . . . [for example] Turks, Greeks, Spaniards, Italians, even all that latitude" (3:61). In addition, Burton writes that this kind of lewd behavior is most often found in the urban centers of these southern nations, so it appears that Calisto's social status and his external environment in *Celestina*'s unnamed Spanish town meet all of the principal requirements for acquiring this terrible illness: "In Italy and Spain they have their stews in every great city . . . every gentleman almost hath a peculiar mistress; fornications, adulteries, are nowhere so common" (3:61). As *Celestina*'s readers would know from Pármeno's detailed description of the old woman's activities in Act I, Burton is correct to observe that "the city is one great bawdy house; how should a man live honest among so much provocation?" (3:61).

Burton's views on Calisto, even though they form only a small part of his extensive analysis of the causes and effects of heroical love, present a unique perspective for modern readers of *Celestina*. As noted in Chapter 5 of the present study, Calisto has often been considered a contradictory or even a ridiculous character by some of the most prominent scholars of the Spanish Renaissance.[7] Significantly, unlike many

---

6. For example, Bernardus Gordonius writes: "E dize se 'hereos': porque los ricos & los nobles por los muchos plazeres que han, acostumbran de caer: o incurrir en esta passion" (qtd. in Seniff 14).

7. See Marcel Bataillon 1961, 109; José Antonio Maravall 19; and James R. Stamm

of Calisto's modern critics, Burton seems to find nothing unusual or unexpected in the young man's behavior. On the contrary, Burton clearly believes that the *galán*'s amorous condition embodies the most common characteristics of love melancholy that have existed in European literature throughout the centuries. Calisto's momentary rapture and overwhelming ardor for Melibea in Act I represent two of the typical attributes of *amor hereos* found among young lovers, and his tragic death at the end of the work serves as a fitting example of the terrible dangers associated with the disease. Although he does not condone Calisto's exaggerated lovesick behavior, in *The Anatomy* he indicates that the young protagonist's social and national background offers few alternatives to the horrendous suffering of erotic melancholy. Under the societal and personal conditions that Burton describes, Calisto appears to be an innocent victim of the malady rather than the parodic or absurd character often described by modern critics.

Celestina, like Calisto, is mentioned four times in *The Anatomy*. The first reference to the old bawd appears in the Second Partition ("The Cure of Melancholy"), in a section titled "Retention and Evacuation Rectified." In this section, Burton discusses the benefits of sexual relations, which according to some medical authorities reduce anger and alleviate melancholy. A complete lack of sex, on the other hand, creates an excess of harmful vapors in the brain that—in the words of Valescus—makes "the mind sad [and] the body dull and heavy" (2:33). More important, sexual abstinence produces the retention of seed in both men and women (2:33), a physical condition that may lead to madness. According to medical authorities such as Avicenna and Oribasius, this mental illness can then be cured only by active sexual relations.

The reputed benefits of sexual intercourse notwithstanding, Burton notes that many authors strongly criticize this practice as harmful and immoral.[8] Plutarch and Marsilio Ficino, for example, believe that sex can be extremely damaging to the spirit, and Jason Pratensis notes that it should be avoided because it is the source of many serious diseases. Other writers, including Aristotle, indicate that excessive sexual activity is particularly hazardous because it reduces one's life span, as can be seen in some species of birds that are "short-lived because of their

---

39. In addition, Alan Deyermond, June Hall Martin, María Eugenia Lacarra, and Dorothy S. Severin believe that Calisto is an essentially comic character who represents an absurd parody of the literary courtly lover.

8. For other authorities who counsel against excessive sexual intercourse, see Solomon 1997, 55–56.

salacity, which is very frequent" (2:34). Because of these dangers, Ludovicus Antonius prohibits carnal relations in athletes and manual laborers, and "Ficin[o] and Marsilius Cognatus put Venus [as] one of the five mortal enemies of a student: 'It consumes the spirits, and weakens the brain'" (2:33–34).

When faced with this contradictory information about the benefits as well as the potential dangers of venery, Burton adopts a practical approach and recommends a moderate level of sexual activity, although he admits that he is unsure of where this middle ground lies: "The extremes being both bad, the medium is to be kept, which cannot be easily determined" (2:34). Nevertheless, even though every individual has unique physical characteristics that require different levels of carnal relations, Burton concludes that the possibilities of serious harm are minimal: "*Confodi multas enim, occidi vero paucas per ventrem vidisti* (In truth you have seen many injured through the belly, but few slain that way), as that Spanish Cælestina merrily said" (2:34).[9]

Fortunately for Burton's readers, the old bawd confirms that these things are not nearly as bad as some learned scholars make them out to be, which allows for a certain amount of personal discretion in each individual case. It is interesting to note that despite the intellectual prestige of writers such as Aristotle, Plutarch, and the *alter Plato* Marsilio Ficino, Burton ignores their criticism of sexual relations and presents Celestina as the ultimate authority on carnal activity. In fact, Burton concludes that her positive views on sexual relations are more accurate and definitive than those found in the works of illustrious doctors such as Avicenna and Oribasius.

The next two references to Celestina appear in the sections of the Third Partition devoted to the characteristics and causes of heroical love. The first reference is found in the subsection titled "Importunity and Opportunity of Time, Place, Conference, Discourse, Singing, Dancing, Musick, Amorous Tales, Objects, Kissing, Familiarity, Tokens, Presents, Bribes, Promises, Protestations, Tears, &c." Burton writes that men and women often try to win their beloved's affection with presents, promises, and flattery, or in some cases through outright

---

9. This paraphrase alludes to the conversation between Celestina and Pármeno in the first act:

CELESTINA: ¡Mas rabia me mate, si te llego a mí, aunque vieja! Que la voz tienes ronca, las barvas te apuntan; mal sosegadilla deves tener la punta de la barriga.
PÁRMENO: ¡Como cola de alacrán!
CELESTINA: Y aún peor, que la otra muerde sin hinchar, y la tuya hincha por nueve meses. (I, 118)

lies. These schemes are particularly effective with younger and inexperienced lovers who can be easily taken in with this sort of deception. Nevertheless, if these methods fail then the most common stratagem is to fake the tears, sighs, and paleness of erotic melancholy. Although well-planned tricks fool some people, Burton notes, Celestina is perfectly aware that these ruses are nothing more than a provocative affectation because, as far as the old bawd is concerned, one lover is entirely as good as another:

> Thou thinkest . . . because of her vows, tears, smiles, and protestations, she is solely thine . . . when as indeed there is no such matter, as the Spanish bawd said . . . she will have one sweetheart in bed, another in the gate, a third singing at home, a fourth, & c. Every young man she sees she likes hath as much interest, and shall as soon enjoy her as thyself. ["¡Ay, ay (Areúsa), si viesses el saber de tu prima (Elicia) y qué tanto le ha aprovechado mi criança y consejos . . . ! Y aunque no se halla ella mal con mis castigos, que uno en la cama y otro en la puerta, y otro que sospira por ella en su casa se precia de tener" (VII, 205).] (3:125)

Celestina is also mentioned in the next subsection, titled "Bawds, Philters, Causes," although she surprisingly merits but one brief reference in this part of *The Anatomy*. Burton believes that once the many allurements listed in the previous section have been exhausted, then the lover's last hope is to enlist the help of a go-between to help resolve his amorous condition. These women are so capable in the discharge of their professional responsibilities that—at least in Burton's view—there is virtually no way for them to fail an assignment: "[N]on est mulieri mulier insuperabilis [There's no woman that a woman can't overcome], Cælestina said, let him or her never be so honest, watched and reserved, 'tis hard but one of these old women will get access" (3:127). ("Que aunque esté brava Melibea, no es ésta . . . la primera a quien yo he hecho perder el cacarrear. . . . Porque sé que aunque al presente la ruegue, al fin me ha de rogar" [III, 144–45].)

Readers of *Celestina* might expect the old woman to play a greater role in the section of the work devoted to bawds, especially with the respect that Burton shows for her knowledge and judgment in other sections of *The Anatomy*. Nevertheless, despite Celestina's obvious talents as a *tercera*, Burton reserves his most profound interest—as well as his greatest venom—for a completely different kind of go-between. According to the Anglican minister Burton, Catholic priests are the most notorious practitioners of this ancient profession, as they are prone to take a more personal interest in their assignments than even the Spanish bawd: "The most sly, dangerous, and cunning bawds, are your knavish physicians, empyrics, Mass-priests, monks, Jesuits, and friars . . . [who] promise to restore maidenheads, and do it without danger, make an abortion if need be . . . hinder conception, procure lust . . . and now and then step in themselves" (2:128). It seems that in Burton's view Celestina is at least true to her word and to her profession, whereas Catholic priests violate their most cherished religious and moral standards because of their uncontrolled sexual passion.

Burton's final reference to Celestina occurs in the Third Partition as part of his analysis of jealousy ("Symptoms of Jealousy: Fear, Sorrow, Suspicion, Strange Actions, Gestures, Outrages, Locking Up, Oaths, Trials, Laws, & c."). Although Burton repeatedly insists on the seriousness of heroical love's myriad symptoms, he believes that jealousy is the worst manifestation of the disease: "'Tis a more vehement passion, a more furious perturbation, a bitter pain, a fire . . . madness, vertigo, plague, hell" (3:280). While this malady causes the lover to "sigh, weep, [and] sob," much as he would while feeling the normal passion of *amor hereos*, the jealous lover also exhibits "those strange gestures of staring, frowning, grinning, rolling of eyes, menacing, ghastly looks" (3:280). Just like the lovesick young man, the jealous man exhibits melancholic behavior that tends to be completely inconsistent, as he roars and complains about his beloved's unfaithfulness one minute, and then suddenly begs her forgiveness the next. Nevertheless, despite this momentary calm in his emotions, nothing can permanently cool his passion or satisfy his insane fixation.[10]

A central part of jealous melancholy is the groom's overriding concern about his bride's virginity. Some European cultures resolve this question publicly by exhibiting the newlyweds' sheets the morning after the wedding, while other, more circumspect nations prefer to conduct a discreet medical examination of the young woman before the ceremony. Notwithstanding these efforts to determine the bride's vir-

---

10. Jealous behavior is more common in men; it is, however, also found in some women. Burton mentions the unusual case of "Joan Queen of Spain, wife to King Philip, mother of Ferdinand and Charles the Fifth, Emperors [*sic*]" (3:282), referring of course to Juana la Loca. According to Burton, the writings of Gómez-Miedes reveal that, despite the pleading of the Archbishop and Isabella the queen mother, Joan "could not contain herself, 'but in a rage ran upon a yellow-haired wench,' with whom she suspected her husband to be naught, 'cut off her hair, did beat her black and blue, and so dragged her about'" (3:282–83). It appears from Juana's example that the southern regions make the women every bit as lusty as the men.

ginity, and therefore her suitability for marriage, Burton indicates that there are many ways to circumvent even the most assiduous vigilance of the young woman's chastity:

> An old bawdy nurse in Aristænetus (like that Spanish Cælestina, *quæ quinque mille virgines fecit mulieres, totidemque mulieres arte sua virgines* [who made women of five thousand virgins, and by her art restored as many women to virginity]), when a fair maid wept . . . how she had been deflowered, and now ready to be married, was afraid it would be perceived, comfortably replied . . . "Fear not, daughter, I'll teach thee a trick to help it." ["Entiendo que passan de cinco mil virgos los que se han hecho y deshecho por su autoridad en esta cibdad" (I, 103).] (3:285)

Judging by his references to the old bawd and to her remarkable abilities, Burton understands that Celestina—just like any other experienced go-between—performs a necessary function for both men and women in contemporary European society. On the one hand, these bawds help young men to fulfill their lovesick desires by communicating with their *amadas* and convincing them to accept the *galán*'s amorous attentions. At the same time, these go-betweens prevent young women from becoming the unfortunate victims of the same irrational sensibilities that produced the man's heroical love in the first place, as they can fake the bride's virginity and thus preserve her possibilities of marriage. More important, Burton—surely one of the most learned scholars on the subject of love melancholy in seventeenth-century Europe—shows clear respect for Celestina's knowledge of amorous relations. While we could logically expect him to criticize the old bawd's immoral activity, he instead quotes her alongside authorities such as Aristotle, Avicenna, and Ficino, and in the end bows to her superior knowledge and experience on the subject of sexual relations.

Although *Celestina* represents only one of the hundreds of source texts that appear in the final edition of *The Anatomy of Melancholy*, Burton's work should be of great interest not only to scholars of the Spanish Renaissance, but more important, also to modern readers of *Celestina*. *The Anatomy* represents one of the first English commentaries on Fernando de Rojas's work, so it has an important historical value relating to the study of Spanish letters in the English-speaking world. In addition, *The Anatomy* places Celestina's professional activities within a wider historical and cultural context, and it shows that her occupation played a vital public role for both men and women in contemporary European society.

Burton also uses the Third Partition of *The Anatomy* to examine the symptoms, causes, and effects of heroical love, which is precisely the unusual and often confusing malady that affects Calisto. Since the *galán* remains a difficult and contradictory character for modern readers of *Celestina*, Burton's study may prove useful in the continuing critical effort to understand the enigmatic nature of the work's young protagonist. At the same time, *The Anatomy of Melancholy* suggests that Calisto is an unwitting victim of erotic melancholy, so there would seem to be nothing unusual or unexpected in his passionate and apparently illogical behavior. From Burton's analysis of the young European *inamorato*, it appears that Calisto's horrible death outside of Melibea's walls should be seen as an example of the tragic results of this terrible disease, which provides one more reason why young men must protect themselves from the scourge of love melancholy.

5

Castiglione's *Il cortegiano* and the Depiction of Sensual Love in *Celestina*

Although Robert Burton considers Calisto to be a typical example of the young European *inamorato, Celestina*'s young protagonist still appears to be the most misunderstood and most criticized character in all of Spanish Renaissance literature. The *galán*'s frequently irrational and inexplicable behavior has made him the butt of criticism and unfavorable comments, not only on the part of the work's other characters, but also from some of *Celestina*'s most distinguished modern commentators. This negative viewpoint appears somewhat understandable if we consider that Calisto lives out an enigmatic existence in the darkness of his own bedroom, a private place where he spends many of his days and nights reciting amorous verse and lamenting his apparently impossible love for Melibea. He is so out of touch with external reality that he remains absolutely oblivious to the obvious deception of his two servants Sempronio and Pármeno, and he later shows only brief remorse when he learns that they have been executed after murdering Celestina. Worse yet, Calisto also seems to be excessively hasty when he consumes his passionate love for Melibea in the young woman's garden, and this same recklessness leads to his death without confession when he falls outside of her walls during the *Comedia*'s third evening.

If we take into account Calisto's unusual and erratic behavior, it is unsurprising that Sempronio calls his master a "loco" (I, 92), "herege" (I, 92), "necio" (I, 101), and even "hydeputa" (VIII, 218). In addition, shortly after meeting Calisto for the first time, Celestina tells Pármeno that "éste tu amo, como dizen, me paresce rompenecios" (I, 122). Even Pármeno—who is much younger and more ingenuous than the experienced Sempronio—indicates at the beginning of the work that his master is the "[d]iestro cavallero . . . Calisto" (I, 108), but he soon realizes that the *galán* is little more than a frivolous and irresponsible young man. More important, Calisto seems to produce the same negative reaction in his beloved Melibea. Despite the *galán*'s ardent love for the young woman, Melibea tells Celestina in the fourth act that Calisto is a "loco, saltaparedes, fantasma de noche, luengo como cigüeña, figura de paramiento malpintado" (IV, 162).[1]

Many of *Celestina*'s modern critics share the generally negative view of Calisto that is frequently expressed by the work's other characters. Marcel Bataillon (1961), for example, believes that this "amoreux foux" is "plus digne de risée que de sympathie" (109). José Antonio Maravall (1964) also writes that Calisto "responde fielmente a la figura del joven miembro de la clase ociosa" (32), and that "el desorden interno que este personaje pone de manifiesto afecta . . . a todos los estratos de la sociedad" (19). Alan Deyermond (1961), June Hall Martin (1972), María Eugenia Lacarra (1989), and Dorothy S. Severin (1989) all agree that Calisto is an essentially foolish character who represents an absurd, comic parody of the literary courtly lover. James R. Stamm (1988) adds that Calisto is "libresco e ingenuo, algo pusilánime y poco decidido" (39), as well as "grosero, frío y egoísta" (141).

In contrast to the repeated criticism of *Celestina*'s young protagonist, other scholars adopt a more moderate position on Calisto, although always with a clear recognition of the *galán*'s problematical and contradictory personality. María Rosa Lida de Malkiel (1962) writes that "la nota básica de Calisto es su egoísmo" (347), but at the same time she emphasizes the young man's imaginative and literary quali-

---

1. It is important to remember that, despite this apparent criticism, Melibea's harsh words about Calisto are likely meant to conceal her love for Calisto. See Shipley 1975 and my *Calisto's Dream* (1995, 103–10) for two analyses of how Melibea participates in Celestina's deception during their conversation in Act IV. More important, Miguel Garci-Gómez concludes that Melibea's apparently critical words in Act IV in reality reveal the young woman's passion for Calisto (see Chapter 1, n. 9 above).

ties. Peter N. Dunn (1975) also recognizes Calisto's many defects, but he observes that we lack a complete understanding of the *galán*'s character because we only see him in the midst of an amorous passion that represents "a symbolic reversal of what love should achieve" (112). Dunn notes that in Dante's *La vita nuova*, the Italian poet is ennobled by his platonic love for Beatrice, but Calisto's ardent love for Melibea instead accentuates the *inamorato*'s fantasy and lack of judgment: "[Calisto's] passion, far from endowing him with any higher understanding, has deprived him of the most common understanding. Reversing day and night, unaware of either time or necessity, he is removed from the world's natural pulse and rhythm. He can respond to nothing but the flux of feeling and the allurements of fantasy" (113).

I have also analyzed Calisto's contradictory character (1991, 1995), but I question the idea that the *galán* could be a mere parody of the literary courtly lover. Calisto clearly embodies many of the characteristics of the courtly lover presented in Andreas Capellanus's *De amore*, a similarity that suggests that the young protagonist is not the absurd caricature previously described by Deyermond, Martin, Lacarra, and Severin. While Calisto's unusual behavior exemplifies the strange symptoms of *amor hereos*, I agree with Lida de Malkiel that the *galán* exhibits a high level of imagination and creativity, a characteristic that takes him far beyond the medieval literary model.

While several generations of Hispanists have interpreted Calisto from a number of different perspectives, the many contradictions that exist in contemporary criticism reveal that modern scholars have not yet resolved the inconsistencies that the *galán* manifests throughout the work. Moreover, although modern critics emphasize Calisto's troubled mental state, it is important to remember that *Celestina* presents another perspective on the young protagonist that most critics have simply ignored. Despite Melibea's bitter words about Calisto in Act IV, shortly before her death the young woman affirms that Calisto was "el más noble cuerpo y más fresca juventud que al mundo era en nuestra edad criada" (XX, 333). Celestina and the two servants often speak of the *galán*'s absurd and foolish character, but Melibea insists that the "virtudes y bondad [de Calisto] a todos eran manifiestas" (XX, 333), almost as though she were speaking about a completely different person. In addition, instead of denying the ardent love that she feels for Calisto, the young woman tells her father that she wants to share her final resting place on earth with her absent lover. In much the same way that the two deaths without confessions will join them in eternal damnation, Melibea requests "que sean juntas nuestras sepulturas; juntas nos hagan nuestras obsequias" (XX, 334).

It is certainly possible that Melibea's parting words about Calisto simply reflect the emotional trauma that she feels following her lover's tragic and untimely death, but the ideas that she expresses shortly before her suicide reflect the same ardent emotions that the young woman has felt at least since Act X. It is also conceivable that Melibea's amorous passion for Calisto has blinded her to the young protagonist's many defects, but the aristocratic background that she mentions during Act XX places him in a well-defined social framework that would preclude such biting criticism of the *joven caballero*. As we can see from Melibea's final words to her father, Pleberio also knew Calisto and his family quite well, and he would therefore be aware of the *galán*'s many noble and admirable qualities: "Muchos días son passados, padre mío, que penava por mi amor un cavallero que se llamava Calisto, el qual tú bien conosciste. Conosciste assimismo sus padres y claro linaje" (XX, 333).

Although some critics may doubt the veracity of Melibea's final words about Calisto in Act XX, the work's thematic unity also contradicts the strong criticism that has been repeatedly expressed about the young protagonist. We must remember that if we accept the negative view of Calisto that is often presented in modern scholarship, then there is no way to explain why a presumably beautiful and intelligent young woman would fall in love with—and then later kill herself over—a young man whom critics believe to be crazy, disorderly, lazy, cowardly, uncouth, and parodic. If we consider the severity of these judgments, then we must conclude that the typical modern reading of Calisto represents an important contradiction not only with respect to Melibea's final words in Act XX, but also with respect to the entire *enredo amoroso* that determines the work's dramatic development.

For modern scholars who have been unable to resolve the apparent contradictions that exist in Calisto's puzzling nature, Baldassare Castiglione's *Il libro del cortegiano* offers a possible key to a greater understanding of the young protagonist's problematical personality. At the end of *Il cortegiano*, the character of the poet Pietro Bembo provides a description of contemporary European *inamorati* that explains much of Calisto's enigmatic and confusing behavior. Castiglione— through Bembo's dialogue—accepts the distinction that Plato establishes between spiritual and mundane pleasures, and he indicates that young men have the tragic tendency to lose themselves in strictly sensual desires. Describing an evident contrast with the nature of the courtesan or of the mature and rational man, Castiglione writes that "la natura umana nella età giovenile ... è inclinata al senso ... [e il cortegiano] deve esser ben cauto e guardarsi di non ingannar se stesso, lassandosi indur in quelle calamità che ne' giovani meritano più compassione che biasimo" (339) ("the nature of man in youthfull age is so much inclined to sense . . . [and the courtier] ought to be good and circumspect, and heedful that he beeguyle not him self, to be lead willfullye into the wretchednesse, that in yonge men deserveth more to be pitied then blamed" [352]).[2]

Much like Plato, Castiglione believes that true beauty is found only in the human soul, and as a result of this fundamental distinction, he concludes, the desire to satisfy a strictly physical attraction is a base and undignified sentiment in any man. Since authentic loveliness is incorporeal by its very nature, the rational man cannot gratify the desire to possess true beauty though the "falso giudicio del senso" (LII, 331) ("false opinyon by the longinge of sense" [344]). On the contrary, sensuality and other physical pleasures are sordid cravings that man shares with the animals, while the use of reason—a higher intellectual faculty found only in human beings—makes man reject these base desires and instead strive for real understanding. According to Castiglione, the faculty of understanding rejects all material pleasures, and instead longs for the "contemplazion di cose intelligibili, quella voluntà solamente si nutrisce di beni spirituali" (LI, 330) ("to beehoulde thinges that may be understoode, so is that wil only fead with spirituall goodes" [343]).[3]

Castiglione also follows the Platonic ideal that a man in love should never establish a purely physical relationship with his beloved. Instead, he should be content to observe her lovely image and listen to the sound of her beautiful voice. The young man who ignores this sage advice and gives in to physical love will not only lose the full use of the faculty of reason, but more important, he will infect the soul with these false and ignoble desires:

2. In *Celestina*, Sempronio also recognizes that Calisto's lack of judgment and reason in Act I is caused by his youth. Sempronio severely criticizes all of the supposed faults he finds in women, among them the fact that "[n]o tienen modo, no razón, no intención" (I, 98). Nevertheless, when Calisto responds that this reproach simply makes him love Melibea more, Sempronio adds: "No es este juyzio para moços, según veo, que no se saben a razón someter; no se saben administrar" (I, 99).

In addition, Celestina confirms Castiglione's idea that sensual delight is far more prevalent among young men: "Por deleyte: semejable es, como seáys [Sempronio y Pármeno] en edad dispuestos para todo linaje de plazer, en que más los moços que los viejos se juntan, assí como para jugar, para vestir, para burlar, para comer y bever, para negociar amores junctos de compaña" (I, 124).

3. *Intelligibili* corresponds to the definition of *inteligible* found in the dictionary of the Real Academia Española: "Dícese de lo que es materia de puro conocimiento, sin intervención de los sentidos" (2:1177).

> [R]itrovandosi [l'anima] summersa nella pregion terrena [il corpo] e . . . priva della contemplazion spirituale, no po da sé intender chiaramente la veritá . . . e perché [i sensi] son fallaci, la empiono d'errori e false opinioni. Onde quasi sempre occorre che i giovani sono avvolti in questo amor sensuale in tutto rubello dalla ragione. (332)
>
> ([F]or when [the soul] seeth her selfe drowned in the earthly prison [of the body] . . . she can not of her self understand plainly at the first the truth. . . . and bicause [the senses] be deceitfull they fyll her with errours and false opinions. Wherupon most communlye it happeneth, that yonge men be wrapped in this sensual love, which is a very rebell against reason. [345])

Calisto's behavior in *Celestina* confirms Castiglione's portrait of the foolish young lover who is deprived of the faculty of reason because of his overpowering sensual desires. Although modern scholars may find Calisto's behavior to be unusual or confusing, in reality this behavior would not surprise contemporary readers because it directly corresponds to the norms for young *inamorati* that Castiglione repeatedly reprimands. According to the Italian writer,

> Questi tali inamorati adunque amano infelicissimamente, perché o vero non conseguono mai li desidèri loro, il che è grande infelicità . . . perché . . . altro non si sente già mai che affanni, tormenti, dolori, stenti, fatiche; di modo che l'esser pallido, afflitto, in continue lacrime e sospiri, il star mesto, il tacer sempre o lamentarsi, il desiderar di morire . . . son le condicioni che si dicono convenir agli inamorati. (332)
>
> (These kind of lovers therfore love most unluckely, for eyther they never comebye their covetinges, whiche is a great unluckinesse . . . [because] there is never other thinge felt, but afflictions, tourmentes, greeffes, pining, travaile, so that to be wann, vexed with continuall teares, and sighes, to lyve with a discontented minde, to be alwaies dumbe, or to lament, to covet death . . . are the properties which they saye beelonge to lovers. (344–45)]

Without question, this description of the characteristics of the young lover provides an accurate depiction of the psychic conditions that affect Calisto at the beginning of *Celestina*. Starting in the anonymous first act, the *galán* recognizes that he suffers this internal confusion precisely because he lacks the full control of the faculty of reason: "¿Cómo templará el destemplado? ¿Cómo sentirá el armonía aquel que consigo está tan discorde, aquel en quien *la voluntad a la razón no obedece*? Quien tiene dentro del pecho aguijones, paz, guerra, tregua, amor, enemistad, injurias, peccados, sospechas, todo a una causa" (I, 91; emphasis added). In addition, as we can see from Sempronio's words to Calisto at the beginning of Act II, the young man experiences the precise symptoms of the uncontrolled passion that Castiglione believes must be avoided by the Renaissance courtesan: "Señor . . . en viéndote solo, dizes desvaríos de hombre sin seso, sospirando, gemiendo, maltrobando, holgando con lo oscuro, desseando soledad, buscando nuevos modos de pensativo tormento, donde, si perseveras, o de muerto o loco no te podrás escapar" (II, 132).

Calisto has reached this bleak predicament because, instead of satisfying himself with seeing Melibea's image and listening to her mellifluous voice, he demonstrates from the very beginning of the work that he wants to establish a purely carnal relationship with the young woman. In fact, the sensual quality of Calisto's love for her is so strong that it even dominates the young man's dreamworld imagination, as revealed when Celestina brings Melibea's cordon to the young man's house in Act VI. Castiglione writes that the *inamorato* should "godasi con gli occhi . . . [e] con l'audito" because "questi dui sensi . . . tengon poco del corporeo e son ministri della ragione" (340) ("injoye wyth his eyes . . . [and] with hearinge . . . [because] these two senses, which have litle bodelye substance in them . . . be the ministers of reason" [353]).[4] While Calisto obviously enjoys the sight of Melibea's cordon, he wants his other senses to share the experience of the beauty of this almost sacred relic: "Y mándame mostrar aquel santo cordón que tales miembros fue digno de ceñir. Gozarán mis ojos con todos los otros sentidos, pues juntos han sido apassionados" (VI, 185). More important, when Calisto tells Celestina that he often sees the young woman in his nighttime imagination, he reveals that these nocturnal fantasies are also characterized by an undeniable sensual quality. In Calisto's dreams, "Todos los sentidos le llagaron [a mi lastimado coraçón]; todos acor-

---

4. Like much of this section of *Il cortegiano*, this analysis of the senses is derived from Marsilio Ficino's *Commentary on Plato's Symposium*, which was finished sometime between 1474 and 1475. According to Ficino, "[I]t is apparent to anyone that of those six powers of the soul, three pertain to body and matter, that is, touch, taste, and smell; but the other three, that is, reason, sight, and hearing, pertain to the soul. . . . [T]he three higher senses, most remote from the material . . . perceive those things which move the body very little, but the soul very much" (part V, 166). See also Lorenzo de' Medici's commentary to his own Sonnet VIII (96).

rieron a él con sus esportillas de trabajo; cada uno le lastimó quanto más pudo; los ojos en vella, los oýdos en oýlla, las manos en tocalla" (VI, 185).

While Castiglione writes that the loss of reason affects the *inamorato*'s judgment and self-control, he also discusses the physical and spiritual results of erotic melancholy. According to the Italian writer, every *inamorato* feels a "mirabil diletto" (343) ("wonderous delite" [356]) inside of his body, a pleasant sensation that creates an inner heat around the heart that in turn melts "alcune virtù sopite e congelate nell'anima" (343) ("certain virtues in a trance and congealed in the soule" [356]). Once these forces are unfrozen in the soul, they cause the eyes to emit "vivi spiriti" (340) ("livelye spirites" [353]) or *pneuma* that according to Castiglione consists of "vapori sotilissimi, fatti della più pura e lucida parte del sangue, i quali ricevono la imagine della bellezza e la formano con mille varii ornamenti" (343) ("fyne vapoures made of the purest and cleerest parte of the bloode, which receive the image of the beawtie, and decke it with a thousande sundrye fournitures" [356]).[5]

The young man's pleasure at perceiving the visual image of his beloved through these sanguinary spirits creates feelings of delight and surprise that affect the soul as much as the body: "[L]'anima si diletta e con una certa maraviglia si spaventa e pur gode e, quasi stupefatta, insieme col piacere sente quel timore e riverenzia che alle cose sacre aver si sòle e parle d'esser nel suo paradiso" (343) ("Wherupon the soule taketh a delite, and with a certein wonder is agast, and yet enjoyeth she it, and [as it were] astonied together with the pleasure, feeleth the feare and reverence that men accustomably have towarde holy matters, and thinketh her self to be in paradise" [356–57]).

Castiglione's depiction of the young man admiring the visual image of his *amada* provides an accurate description of Calisto's wonder and delight while observing Melibea's image in *Celestina*'s opening scene. Although the *galán* does not observe her material presence, he is absolutely overcome by the young woman's overpowering beauty, because he beholds a likeness that he believes to be superior to the divine vision of the saints in heaven. As Calisto notes when he observes her beautiful image in the work's opening scene, "En esto veo, Melibea, la grandeza de Dios. . . . Por cierto, los gloriosos santos que se deleytan en la visión divina no gozan más que yo agora en el acatamiento tuyo. . . . [E]n verdad, que si Dios me diesse en el cielo la silla sobre sus santos, no lo ternía por tanta felicidad" (I, 85–88).

5. This description of the *pneuma*, or the spirit that joins and provides communication between the soul and the body, is also derived from Marsilio Ficino (see Couliano 28).

Although Calisto feels an unbridled joy in Melibea's vision at the beginning of *Celestina*'s first scene, Castiglione indicates that the young man who experiences a strictly carnal desire for his beloved enjoys but a momentary emotional pleasure in her presence. Despite the elation that the lover experiences while observing his *amada*'s image, Castiglione writes, he will feel almost blind once he loses this visual contact with her: "L'amante adunque che considera la bellezza solamente nel corpo, perde questo bene e questa felicità sùbito che la donna amata, assentandosi, lassa gli occhi senza il suo splendore e, conseguentemente, l'anima viduata del suo bene" (343) ("The lover therfore that considereth only the beawtie in the bodye, loseth this treasure and happinesse, assoone as the woman beloved with her departure leaveth the eyes without their brightnes, and consequently the soule, as a window without her joye" [357]). According to Castiglione's description of the visual phenomenon of love melancholy, the *inamorato* is immediately deprived of the splendor of his beloved's image as soon as he loses sight of her, a result that is confirmed by Calisto's words to Sempronio at the beginning of the second scene of Act I: "Cierra la ventana y dexa la tiniebla acompañar al triste y al desdichado la ceguedad. Mis pensamientos tristes no son dignos de luz" (I, 88).

When Calisto observes the illusory image of Melibea during *Celestina*'s opening scene, he is ecstatic, for his physiological condition mimics the effects of the live spirits that would exit the *galán*'s eyes during an actual encounter with his *amada*. Nevertheless, once Calisto awakens and realizes that he has lost visual contact with her, Castiglione believes that these sanguinary spirits,

> trovando le vie otturate, non hanno esito, e pur cercano d'uscire, e così con quei stimuli rinchiusi pungon l'anima e dànnole passione acerbissima, come a' fanciulli quando dalle tener gingive cominciano a nascere i denti. E di qua procedono le lacrime, i sospiri, gli affani e i tormenti degli amanti; perche l'anima sempre s'affligge e travaglia. (343–44)

> (fyndinge the wayes closed up, have no yssue, and still they seeke to gete out, and so with those shootinges inclosed pricke the soule, and tourment her bitterlye, as yonge chilldren, whan in their tender gummes they beegin to breede teeth. And hens come the teares, sighes, vexations and tourmentes of lovers: bicause the soule is alwayes in affliction and travaile. [357])

This passage in *Il cortegiano* offers a possible explanation for the repeated criticism leveled at Calisto by Celestina, Sempronio, and

Pármeno. With the exception of Act XII, when Sempronio and Pármeno accompany their master during his meeting with Melibea outside of her window, Celestina and the two servants never see Calisto in the company of his beloved. It is therefore perfectly logical that the young protagonist would act like a lovesick fool in their presence because he is always separated from visual contact with Melibea. Nevertheless, under no circumstances should modern readers conclude that this emotional condition is the only facet of Calisto's complex personality. As Dunn has correctly noted, we only see the young protagonist in the midst of an uncontrolled erotic passion, and it is important to remember that the sensual quality of this love produces constant variations in Calisto's psychological condition.

Even though the young protagonist suffers greatly when he is away from Melibea, Castiglione writes, the sensual qualities of this passion cause the *inamorato*'s irrational behavior to vary unexpectedly from one moment to the next. For example, the Italian writer indicates that despite the anguish and the amorous laments that lovesick young men often exhibit, the lover's conduct changes completely once he reestablishes visual contact with his *amada*: "[L]'anima . . . quasi diventa furiosa, fin che quella cara belleza se le appresenta un'altra volta; ed allor sùbito s'acqueta e respira ed a quella tutta intenta si nutrisce di cibo dulcissimo, né mai da così suave spettacolo partir vorria" (344) ("[T]he soul . . . wexeth woode, untill the beloved beawtie commeth beefore her once again, and then is she immediatlye pacified and taketh breth, and throughlye bent to it, is nouryshed wyth most deintye foode, and by her will, would never depart from so sweete a sight" [357]).

According to this pattern of lovesick behavior, Melibea would believe that Calisto is indeed the "más acabado hombre que en gracias nació" (XX, 333)—despite all of the irrational conduct that he exhibits in front of Celestina and his two servants—because the young protagonist changes his lovesick comportment whenever he finds himself in her presence. The apparent contradiction that exists between Melibea's vision of Calisto and the perspective of the three other characters is therefore resolved, since the young woman does not see the *galán* in the midst of the absurd suffering and lamentations that affect him at the beginning of the work.[6] As we have seen, Castiglione writes that

6. The only time that Calisto cries in Melibea's presence is in Act XII, but it is because he initially believes that Celestina has lied to him about the young woman's love for him. Melibea immediately realizes that these tears do not represent any absurd sobbing, but are rather a sure proof of the depths of the *galán*'s love: "Cessen, señor mío, tus verdaderas querellas que ni mi coraçón basta para las sofrir, ni mis ojos para lo dissimular. Tú lloras de tristeza juzgándome cruel; yo lloro de plazer viéndote tan fiel" (XII, 260–61).

the soul "s'acqueta e respira" (344) ("is . . . pacified and taketh breth" ([357]) when it finally returns to the beloved's presence. Calisto feels this same inner peace after he visits Melibea during the work's second evening because he now knows that he will be able to see her whenever he wishes. As the *galán* indicates when he awakens the next morning, "¡O cómo he dormido tan a mi plazer después de aquel açucarado rato, después de aquel angélico razonamiento! Gran reposo he tenido; el sosiego y descanso ¿proceden de mi alegría, o lo causó el trabajo corporal, mi mucho dormir, o la gloria y plazer del ánimo?" (XIII, 275–76).

Although Calisto exhibits a new and more positive attitude during the work's third morning, Celestina, Sempronio, and Pármeno never see this variation in his character because the three of them die before Calisto's early-morning soliloquy. It appears that by paying so much attention to the three characters' critical comments about Calisto, many modern scholars have lost the opportunity to observe a notable change in the *galán*'s behavior beginning in Act XII. The Calisto that we see at the start of *Celestina* often appears to be a laughable or perhaps deranged character, but Castiglione's work suggests that this is not the *galán*'s true nature, but rather a sudden change that takes place because the young man lacks the reason and worldly experience that he needs to defend himself from the terrible temptation of physical love.[7]

Although some modern critics see Calisto as a one-dimensional and parodic character, it is important to remember that *Celestina* confirms Dunn's observation that Calisto's amorous condition does not represent the young protagonist's true disposition. Sempronio's aside in the third scene of Act I reveals that the *galán* has recently suffered a significant alteration in his disposition, and that this change has been as sudden as it is unexpected: "(¡O desventura, o súbito mal! ¿Quál fue tan contrario acontescimiento que ansí tan presto robó el alegría de este

---

7. Although Castiglione believes that young men do not possess full use of the faculty of reason, the Italian writer also indicates that there are physiological reasons for the sensual love that often affects young people. As we have seen, the live spirits that establish visual contact with the beloved are made up of the purest part of the blood. It is believed that young people have lighter blood because the bloodstream fills with impurities over time. The lighter blood heats up quickly, so it is easier to project the live spirits through the young person's eyes. Older people not only develop a more complete use of reason, but also possess heavier blood that becomes heated with more difficulty. Celestina uses a proverb to express a similar idea to Melibea in Act IV, and also to calm the young woman's fury: "Mientra viviere tu yra más dañará mi descargo; que estás muy rigurosa y no me maravillo, que la sangre nueva poco calor ha menester para hervir" (IV, 163). See also a similar analysis of the condition of the blood in the young and old in Ficino's *Commentary* (part VII, 221–22).

hombre, y lo que peor es, junto con ella el seso?)" (I, 89). Nevertheless, once Calisto admits to Sempronio that he is madly in love with Melibea, the servant immediately recognizes the symptoms of the young man's erotic melancholy: "No es más menester; bien sé de qué pie coxqueas; yo te sanaré" (I, 93).

Castiglione's analysis of contemporary *inamorati* also explains the contrast that Dunn has noted between Dante's and Calisto's lovesick behavior. Dante follows the Platonic traditions of the Italian Renaissance, so he is content to merely observe his beloved Beatrice in church or in the street; as a result, his love for her does not diminish even though he does not see her for a period of nine years.[8] The poet's chaste and spiritual love for his lady allows him to move up the rungs of the *scala amoris*, the Renaissance ladder of love that improves and transforms the lover through the constant spiritual contemplation and service of his beloved.[9] Calisto, on the other hand, experiences a purely carnal passion for Melibea, which means that the *galán* would never feel ennobled by this amorous passion. Calisto's love cannot "endo[w] him with any higher understanding" (Dunn 113) because this sensual desire deprives him of the use of reason and does not permit him to attain the understanding that is so important under these difficult circumstances.

Despite the lack of logic and comprehension that Calisto exhibits during his periods of erotic melancholy, the tragedy of his death is even

---

8. On the contrary, under the traditions of courtly love and the *dolce stil nuovo*, the very separation from the beloved increases the depth of suffering and intensifies the *inamorato*'s amorous passion (see Couliano 18–19, 22). Calisto's sensual passion in *Celestina* is clearly different from the contemporary Neoplatonic tradition in Renaissance Italy in that the *galán* seeks the physical release for his lovesickness that faithful courtly lovers assiduously avoid. According to Neoplatonic writers such as Ficino, Calisto's attraction for Melibea would not be considered love at all but rather madness, as the true lover satisfies himself with the mental contemplation of his beloved (Ficino 1944, part II, 146–47).

9. A fundamental part of the *scala amoris* is the belief that both lovers are transformed through a shared sense of spiritual perfection. According to Lorenzo de' Medici, for example, "[C]hi propone uno vero amore, di necessità propone grande perfezzione ... così nello amato come in chi ama" (36) ("[W]hoever posits true love of necessity posits great perfection ... both in the beloved and the lover" [37]). Lorenzo believes that in order to attain the "perfezzione d'amore che si chiama 'sommo bene'" ("perfection of love that one calls 'the highest good'"), the beloved must possess "somma perfezzione" ("the highest perfection"), which includes "ingegno grande, modi e costumi ornati e onesti, maniera e gesti eleganti, destrezza d'accorte e dolci parole, amore, constanzia e fede" (36) ("great liveliness of mind, graceful and chaste behavior and habits, an elegant manner and actions, wise adroitness and sweet words, and love, constancy, and faith" [37]). While Melibea possesses most of these qualities, her sensual passion precludes the *costumi ornati e onesti*, which means that she is incapable of inspiring Calisto's spiritual development.

greater because the *galán* must have been a noble and honorable young man before falling in love.[10] He was certainly the "[d]iestro cavallero" that Párneno mentions in the first act (I, 108), a characterization that is verified by Melibea's description of the terrible results of his death. It is obvious from her words in Act XX that Calisto was neither a fool nor an idiot, and much less an absurd or parodic character. Instead, he was a young aristocrat who exemplified the "gentileza," "cortesía," and "virtud" (XX, 333) that were expected of this powerful social class in Renaissance Europe:

> Yo cobrí de luto y xergas en este día quasi la mayor parte de la cibdadana cavallería; yo dexé [hoy] muchos sirvientes descubiertos de señor; yo quité muchas raciones y limosnas a pobres y envergonçantes. Yo fui la ocasión que los muertos toviessen compañía del más acabado hombre que en gracias nació. Yo quité a los vivos el dechado de gentileza, de invenciones galanas, de atavíos y bordaduras, de habla, de andar, de cortesía, de virtud. Yo fui causa que la tierra goze sin tiempo el más noble cuerpo y más fresca juventud que al mundo era en nuestra edad criada. (XX, 333)

Critics who take an excessively negative view of Calisto adopt this position because they overlook not only the tragic sentiments expressed by Melibea at the end of the work, but also the young protagonist's many noble qualities. These scholars use the beginning of *Celestina* as virtually their only point of textual reference, and as a result they have formed an incomplete and distorted view of the *galán*. This critical approach denies Calisto the personal development that he exhibits after seeing Melibea for the second time in Act XII, and also fails to consider the social and aristocratic background that defines Calisto as an honored member of the town's "cibdadana cavallería" (XX, 333). Moreover, it is important to remember that if Calisto were truly the absurd and deranged character that modern scholars often describe, then there would be no way to understand the suffering and anguish that Melibea expresses in Act XX, and much less her tragic death without confession.

Castiglione's description of amorous melancholy in *Il cortegiano* offers a unique and more complete understanding of Calisto's character, as well as an apparently logical somatic explanation for his lovesick

---

10. It is also possible that, despite Calisto's positive qualities, his youth makes him *enamoradizo* and frequently subject to these passionate desires. Sempronio, for example, calls him a "philósoph[o] de Cupido" (I, 94), and later tells him: "Ponte pues en la medida de honrra; piensa ser más digno de lo que te reputas" (I, 99).

condition. In addition, Castiglione's analysis of erotic melancholy confirms the more complex view of the *galán* that appears in the work of Lida de Malkiel and Dunn. At the same time, *Il cortegiano* explains the contradictory viewpoints on the *galán* expressed by the work's different characters, as it provides a standard code of conduct for young men who are dominated by sensual passion. Although Castiglione presents important ideas about Calisto's problematical behavior, this contemporary vision of the young lover should not surprise *Celestina*'s modern readers. The presentation of the tragedy of mundane love is precisely what one should expect from *Celestina*, particularly if we consider that Fernando de Rojas's opening comments in "El autor a un su amigo" reveal that the work's didactic purpose is to demonstrate the terrible consequences of the physical love that often affects *mancebos* in fifteenth- and sixteenth-century Spain:

> [A] vezes retraýdo en mi cámara . . . me venía a la memoria no sólo la necessidad que nuestra común patria tiene de la presente obra por la muchedumbre de galanes y enamorados mancebos que posee, pero aun en particular vuestra mesma persona, cuya juventud de amor ser presa se me representa aver visto y dél cruelmente lastimada, a causa de le faltar defensivas armas para resistir sus fuegos, las quales hallé esculpidas en estos papeles, no fabricadas en las grandes herrerías de Milan, mas en los claros ingenios de doctos varones castellanos formadas. (69)

According to Fernando de Rojas's opening words to his unnamed friend, Calisto's enigmatic behavior should not lead *Celestina*'s readers to criticize the young protagonist's foolish and even contradictory character. Instead, the dreadful effects of his amorous passion should produce an absolute condemnation of the tragic effects of the mundane love that is so common among the *muchedumbre de galanes* in contemporary Spain. As noted above, Castiglione believes that the madness of sensual love represents a "calamità che ne' giovani meritano più compassione che biasimo" (339) ("wretchednesse, that in yonge men deserveth more to be pitied then be blamed" [352]), an idea that should be remembered by the many scholars who have repeatedly belittled and ridiculed Calisto. More important, if we prefer to stick to the text of *Celestina*, we may simply recall the old bawd's words to Pármeno about his master's amorous condition: "Has de saber, Pármeno, que Calisto anda de amor quexoso; y no lo juzgues por esso por flaco, que el amor impervio todas las cosas vence" (I, 117).

6

Echando mis sentidos por ventores y my juyzio a bolar

Melancholy and Didacticism in *Celestina*

In the preceding five chapters of this study I have analyzed *Celestina* as part of a European cultural and literary tradition that emphasizes the mundane and physiological basis of the phantasmal dreams and visions of erotic melancholy. Within the specific framework of this legacy, in this final chapter I will demonstrate that *Celestina* is also part of the related tradition in European letters of *reprobatio amoris*, a problem that Rojas describes in "El autor a un su amigo" as "las malas cogitaciones y vicios de amor" (75). Although the question of whether *Celestina* truly exhibits a fundamental didactic character no longer generates the same interest and controversy once found in the works of Marcel Bataillon (1961), María Rosa Lida de Malkiel (1962), and Stephen Gilman (1972),[1] here I will demonstrate that *Celestina*'s textual development repeatedly refers to and insists on its own instructional quality. At the same time, I will examine Fernando de Rojas's

---

1. Bataillon believes that *Celestina* possesses a didactic and moral foundation (1961, 215–25 and 251–68), a position strongly criticized by Lida de Malkiel (292–316) and Gilman (1972, 357–67). Vicente Cantarino provides a useful summary of this controversy (105).

authorial intentions from the perspective of the contemporary theories of melancholy that appear in the preceding chapters of this study.

As noted in Chapter 3, modern scholars agree that *Celestina* begins with the anonymous *papeles* that form the basis of the first act of Fernando de Rojas's *Comedia* and *Tragicomedia de Calisto y Melibea*. Nevertheless, one of the biggest surprises in Charles B. Faulhaber's *Celestina* de Palacio manuscript is that the text includes the *Incipit* and the *Argumento general*—to use the nomenclature developed by Miguel Marciales—both of which were generally believed to be the work of the *bachiller* Rojas.[2] The Palacio version of the *Incipit* indicates that the *Comedia* was "conpuesta en rreprenhension delos locos enamorados que, vençidos en su deshordenado apetito, a sus amigas llaman y dizen ser su dios. Asi mesmo fecha en aviso delos engaños delas alcauetes y malos y lisongeros servientes" (29). The *Incipit* specifically criticizes both the lasciviousness of contemporary *locos enamorados*, as well as the deception that frequently characterizes go-betweens and servants. In addition, the Palacio manuscript's *Argumento general* indicates that lust and greed are directly responsible for the five main characters' *amargo y desastrado fin*,[3] an idea that further emphasizes the *Auto*'s didactic purpose:

> Calisto fue de noble linaje y de claro ingenio, de gentil dispusiçion, de linda criança, dotado de muchas gracias, de estado mediano. Fue preso enel amor de Melibea, muger moça, muy generosa, de alta y serenisima sangre . . . Por soliçitud del pungido Calisto, vençido el casto proposito della,—interviniendo Çelestina, mala y astuta muger, con dos servientes del vençido Calisto, engañados y por esta tornados desleales, presa su fidelidad con anzuelo de cobdiçia y deleite—vinieron los amantes y los que los ministraron, en amargo y desastrado fin. (29)

---

2. The principal surprise in the *Auto*'s possible didactic purpose is that—as Keith Whinnom (1977) has observed—prior to this discovery it appeared that "Act I may well have been intended as the beginning of a genuine *comedia* (that is, a play with a happy ending)" (196). See similar conclusions in Fraker 1966, 524 and Castells 1995, 54.

3. As Bruce Wardropper has noted, the mundane desires of lust and greed were thought to be related: "If one asks oneself what it is that the noble world of Calisto and Melibea, Pleberio and Alisa has in common with the underworld of Sempronio and Párm eno, Celestina and her girls, it is surely cupidity, or, better put in Latin, *cupiditas*—a derivative from *cupido*, with or without the initial capital letter. Classical Latin knew that the excessive appetite for women and money was the same moral error, and did not hesitate to call both manifestations by the same name. The early Christian Church, using the same Latin language, also knew that lust and avarice were the same thing, *cupiditas*" (1964, 149–50).

Although the *Celestina de Palacio* strongly suggests that the *Incipit* and the *Argumento general* were written by the primitive author rather than by Fernando de Rojas, both textual elements are missing from the Burgos *Comedia* of 1499, an edition that contains only the individual *argumentos* to the original sixteen acts. The 1500 Toledo edition of the *Comedia* includes the *Incipit* as well as the *Argumento general*, along with the new "Autor a un su amigo" letter. As noted in Chapter 5, Rojas's opening letter reveals that the two friends' *común patria* needs this instructional work because of "la muchedumbre de galanes y enamorados que posee," a problem that has affected Rojas's unnamed friend "en particular" (69). For this reason, the *bachiller* indicates that the *Comedia* offers these lovesick young men the "defensivas armas" that they require in order to protect themselves from the scourge of passionate love (69).

While Rojas's letter to his friend emphasizes the *Auto*'s preceptive character, the *bachiller* also observes that the primitive text has other important literary and philosophical qualities. Rojas lavishly praises the *Auto*'s "estilo elegante, jamás en nuestra castellana lengua visto ni ovdo" (69), as well as its creative use of proverbs and its combination of *filosophía* and *donayres*:

> [L]eýlo tres o quatro vezes, y tantas quantas más lo leýa, tanta más necessidad me ponía de releerlo y tanto más me agradava, y en su processo nuevas sentencias sentía. Vi no sólo ser dulce en su principal ystoria o ficción toda junta, pero aun de algunas sus particularidades salían fontezicas de filosophía, de otros agradables donayres, de otros avisos y consejos contra lisongeros y malos sirvientes y falsas mugeres hechizeras. Vi que no tenía su firma de autor, pero quienquier que fuese, es digno de recordable memoria por la sotil invención, por la gran copia de sentencias entrexeridas que so color de donayres tiene. Gran filósofo era. (69–70)

Even though Rojas admires the primitive text's writing style, its numerous philosophical observations, and the practical advice that it offers against dishonest servants and *mugeres hechizeras*, the *bachiller* understands that there is an important contradictory element in his continuation of *Celestina*. A didactic work is expected to maintain a serious and reserved tone, but Rojas admits in the letter's acrostic verses that he may have subverted his own constructive purpose by including lascivious material in the *Comedia*'s fifteen new acts:

> Si bien discernéys mi limpio motivo,
> a quál se endereça de aquestos estremos,
> con qual participa, quién rige sus remos,
> amor ya aplazible o desamor esquivo,
> buscad bien el fin de aquesto que escrivo,
> o del principio leed su argumento;
> leeldo y veréys que, aunque dulce cuento,
> amantes, que os muestra salir de cativo.
> Como el doliente que píldora amarga
> o la rescela o no puede tragar,
> métenla dentro del dulce manjar,
> engáñase el gusto, la salud se alarga,
> desta manera mi pluma se embarga,
> imponiendo dichos lascivos, rientes,
> atrae los oýdos de penadas gentes,
> de grado escarmientan y arrojan su carga. (72–73)

As a result of *Celestina*'s combination of contradictory thematic elements, Rojas writes that the *Comedia* represents both a *píldora amarga* as well as a *dulce manjar*. This duality describes the same paradoxical quality that later leads Cervantes to characterize the work as both "divi[no]" and "huma[no]" (32), but Rojas attempts to resolve this contradiction by indicating that the *Comedia*'s true message is found in the *Argumento general* and in the work's final act. Nevertheless, although the *bachiller* makes a spirited defense of the *limpio motivo* that leads him to write the continuation, Rojas's clarification of this point suggests that he understands that *Celestina* is susceptible to multiple readings and interpretations.

Perhaps because of the confusion among the work's first readers, Alonso de Proaza's colophon—also found in the 1500 Toledo edition—reinforces the idea that *Celestina* has a clear didactic purpose. Curiously, Proaza's verses indicates that the work's *lector* should play a direct role in this instructional material. According to the *corrector*, the way that the *lector* reads the work in public not only will help to cure his listeners' lovesickness, but it will also remove the sadness so typical of erotic melancholy. These verses are quite significant because if the *lector* follows Proaza's instructions and emphasizes the work's didactic character, then his reading would naturally influence his listeners' interpretation of the work:

> Pues mucho más puede tu lengua hazer,
> lector, con la obra que aquí te refiero,

> que a un coraçón más duro que azero
> bien la leyendo harás liquescer;
> harás al que ama amar no querer,
> harás no ser triste al triste penado;
> al ques sin aviso harás avisado;
> assí que no es tanto las piedras mover. (345)

Although both the *Auto* and the *Comedia* underline the text's didactic nature, the *Tragicomedia*'s interpolations emphasize the work's preceptive character once again. Rojas makes only minor changes to the opening letter in the *Tragicomedia*, but he adds a final stanza to the accompanying acrostic verses. This strophe includes an additional reference to the disasters of sensual love, and—taking a page from the primitive author's *Argumento general*—reminds the public of the tragic end to Calisto's and Melibea's libidinous infatuation:

> O damas, matronas, mancebos, casados,
> notad bien la vida que aquéstos hizieron;
> tened por espejo su fin qual huvieron,
> a otro que amores dad vuestros cuydados.
> Limpiad ya los ojos, los ciegos errados,
> virtudes sembrando con casto bivir,
> a todo correr devéys de huyr,
> no os lance Cupido sus tiros dorados. (75–76)

Similar ideas are also found in the prologue that first appears in the twenty-one-act *Tragicomedia*. The new prologue begins with the well-known quote taken from Heraclitus: "Todas las cosas ser criadas a manera de contienda o batalla" (77). The notion of "lid y offensión" (77) that Rojas presents in the prologue includes wars, envy, and even the controversy over the *Celestina* text itself, as the *bachiller* reveals that the *Comedia* has led its readers to contrasting interpretations "a sabor de su voluntad" (80). In addition, in one of the many passages of the prologue taken from Petrarca's *De remediis*,[4] Rojas notes that this continuing discord may cause the work's public to misunderstand *Celestina*'s didactic purpose:

> Mayormente pues [la obra] con toda las otras cosas que al mundo son, van debaxo de la vandera desta notable sentencia,

---

4. See Alan Deyermond's *The Petrarchan Sources of* La Celestina (chapter 3, "Borrowings from *De remediis utriusque fortunae*," 50–71).

> 'que aun la mesma vida de los hombres, si bien lo miramos, desde la primera edad hasta que blanquean las casas, es batalla'. Los niños con los juegos, los moços con las letras, los mancebos con los deleytes, los viejos con mill especies de enfermedades pelean y estos papeles con todas las edades. La primera los borra y rompe, la segunda no los sabe bien leer, la tercera, que es la alegre juventud y mancebía, discordia. (80)

In his prologue Rojas recognizes that the *Tragicomedia* will encounter as many different kinds of readers and listeners as the *Comedia* did, the text seeming destined to produce a continual *batalla* among readers of *todas las edades*. For this reason, the *bachiller* concludes that, despite the repeated insistence on the work's instructive purpose, at least some of his public will not appreciate the virtue found in *Celestina*: "Unos les roen los huessos que no tienne virtud, que es la hystoria toda junta, no aprovechándose de las particularidades, haziéndola cuento de camino; otros pican los donayres y refranes comunes, loándolos con toda atención, dexando passar por alto lo que haze más al caso y utilidad suya" (80). Fortunately, Rojas concludes that at least some of the work's readers will benefit from the text, since "aquellos para cuyo verdadero plazer es todo, desechan el cuento de la hystoria para contar, coligen la suma para su provecho, ríen lo donoso, las sentencias y dichos de philósophos guardan en su memoria para trasponer en lugares convenibles a sus autos y propósitos" (80).[5]

Despite Rojas's persistent references to *Celestina*'s instructional quality, there still appears to be as much internal contradiction in the *Tragicomedia*'s prologue as there is in the *Comedia*'s opening letter. In the prologue Rojas insists on the work's "provecho" (80), but he also admits that many of the *Comedia*'s readers and listeners were especially captivated by Calisto's and Melibea's passionate love affair. To satisfy this widespread interest, Rojas bowed to the popular request that he "alargasse en el proceso de su deleyte de sus amantes" (81), which suggests that some readers concluded that the work's *dulce manjar* was far more important—or at least far more enjoyable—than its *píldora amarga*.

---

5. Dorothy Severin comments on this passage in her edition of *Celestina:* "Debemos dudar de la sinceridad del consejo de Rojas si consideramos que la mayor parte de sus aforismos están puestos en boca de personajes corruptos y con propósito cuando menos cuestionables" (80–81 n. 32). While this observation is justifiable, it is important to remember that it is precisely the characters' corruption that leads them inexorably to their *desastrado fin*. As Otis H. Green has written, "[*Celestina*'s] theme is passionate love, and death as the inevitable wages of sin. . . . The book follows this pattern with the greatest fidelity: the lovers are sinners and they must die" (1963, 112).

Perhaps because of the continuing confusion over *Celestina*'s true purpose and meaning, Rojas adds some final verses to the *Tragicomedia* that once again emphasize the lovers' tragic end. Placed just before Proaza's colophon, the three new stanzas reiterate the idea that the work's impure content should not distract from its instructional purpose:

> No dudes ni aya vergüença, lector,
> narra lo lascivo que aquí se te muestra,
> que siendo discreto, verás que muestra
> por donde se vende la honesta lavor. (343–44)[6]

Since Rojas himself acknowledges the many different interpretations that have arisen among the work's first readers and listeners, it is unsurprising that *Celestina*'s combination of lascivious and didactic elements continued to produce new controversies throughout the sixteenth century. One notable example of this dispute is found in Fray Juan de Pineda's *Diálogos de la agricultura cristiana*, published in Salamanca in 1589, a full nine decades after the first known edition of the *Comedia*. Pineda reveals that although *Celestina* contains a level of *práctica carnal* not found even in books of chivalry, many young men continue to justify their reading of the work by repeating Rojas's claim that it teaches them to flee *las carnalidades de los malos hombres y mujeres*:

> Muchas vezes he tenido rehiertas con otros mancebos que veo cargados de *Celestinas* y leerlas hasta las saber de coro; y reprehendidos de mí por ello, se piensan descartar con dezir que allí se enseñan a huir de malas mugeres y a conoscer sus embustes, y que viendo pintadas allí como al natural las carnalidades de los malos hombres y mugeres, darán más en rostro y se apartan dellas mejor... No ay cosa en el mundo tan atractiva aun con sólo pensarla y aun sin ymaginarla, ¿y dezís que la leéis cómo se pone por obra para huirla? Ignorancia de gente sin sentido me parece, y muy peor la lección de *Celestina* que la de los libros

---

6. The Valencia *Tragicomedia* of 1514 includes one additional strophe in Proaza's colophon, directed to the *discreto lector*: "Penados amantes jamás conseguieron / dempresa tan alta tan prompta victoria, / como estos de quien recuenta la hystoria / ni sus grandes penas tan bien succedieron. / Mas como firmeza nunca tovieron / los gozos de aqueste mundo traydor / supplico que llores, discreto lector, / el trágico fin que todos ovieron" (346 n. 33).

de cauallerías, en que no ay la práctica carnal, y ay otras virtudes muy platicadas, como lo de la honrra, verdad, amistad, criança y generosidad. (qtd. in Lida de Malkiel 295)

Despite Pineda's bitter criticism of *Celestina*, his own observations suggest that many of Salamanca's *mancebos*—who represent the ideal reading public for the tragic lessons of love melancholy—apparently accepted *Celestina*'s stated didactic purpose. Pineda may decry this interpretation as sheer "ignorancia de gente sin sentido," but it may simply be that these young men needed the text's *defensivas armas* far more than the Salmantine friar. Nevertheless, it is interesting to note that only one page after quoting Pineda's observation that many *mancebos* readily accepted the work's *píldora amarga*, Lida de Malkiel comments: "*La Celestina* constituiría el raro caso de una obra didáctica cuya fundamental inatención está tan bien velada que escapó a la mayoría de los lectores de su siglo y de los siglos siguientes—lo cual implica el más rotundo fracaso didáctico" (296). Even though the Argentine scholar cites such authors as Vives and Cervantes "que en la práctica están muy lejos de considerarla obra moral" (296), it seems that many Spanish *mancebos* were much more receptive to the work's instructional nature—perhaps from practical necessity—than contemporary religious writers and scholars.

Celestina clearly produced differing readings and interpretations beginning with the first editions of the *Comedia*, but this ambiguous quality is part of the text's enduring appeal. There is no question that *Celestina*, like any other major literary work, engages the reader in part because the text is open to multiple interpretations. Nevertheless, it is important to ask if *Celestina* truly produces a spirited and constructive multiplicity of critical readings about the work's didactic character, or if instead the text is marred by the main author's contradictory or perhaps mutually exclusive intentions. More specifically, we may wonder whether the *dulce manjar* that Fernando de Rojas describes in the acrostic verses inadvertently negates or at least contradicts the *píldora amarga* that he supposedly presents as the work's principal remedy against the perils of mundane *deleite*.

The answer to this quandary perhaps lies in the same literary and cultural traditions examined in the preceding chapters of this study. It is important to note that many doctors and philosophers from the classical period to the Renaissance not only explored the symptoms and effects of *amor hereos* in young men, but also discussed and analyzed the many possible cures for this disease. In other words, the *defensivas armas* that Fernando de Rojas found in the anonymous *Celestina* manuscript represent a common element in numerous medical, philosophical, literary, and religious texts throughout the centuries. Moreover, although it would surely surprise Juan de Pineda, Mary Frances Wack's recent research has demonstrated that lascivious activity was one of the most frequent cures for lovesickness in early modern Europe. According to Wack,

> Therapeutic intercourse seems to have posed no ethical dilemma to most of the doctors who wrote on lovesickness, most likely because it fit lay European sexual morality: men's sexual activity outside marriage, especially with prostitutes, seems not to have been viewed very seriously. . . . The easy availability of prostitutes, at least in the larger urban centers where academic physicians, medical students, and their well-to-do patients congregated, suggests that there would have been little practical difficulty in carrying out this cure. . . .
>
> In particular Gerard [of Berry] recommends (again following Avicenna) consorting with and embracing girls, multiple intercourse with them and switching to new ones. Jacques Despars, an expositor of Avicenna, clarifies the relation of this cure to law and faith. "Insani amantes" can make love with those whom the law permits: prostitutes, public women, and slaves . . . but not virgins, religious women, married women, or close relatives. In terms that smack of a connoisseur's appraisal, he specifies that the "bought women" ought to be slim, beautiful, clean, "full of juice" ("succi plenas") and animated. (41, 68)[7]

While the tradition of therapeutic intercourse appears to be completely offensive from a Christian or moral perspective, from a philosophical or medical viewpoint this ethical concern is subordinate to the strictly objective problem of remedying the effects of *amor hereos*. Most of the standard cures for the disease—such as extended travel, pleasant music, hunting, drinking, and a proper diet—would find little objection from religious and moral writers. Nevertheless, *Celestina*'s lascivious content seems like *peccata minuta* in comparison to other contemporary treatments for lovesickness. The 1495 Spanish translation of Bernardus de Gordonius's *Lillio de Medicina*, for example, offers

---

7. The therapeutic intercourse for lovesickness naturally recalls Celestina's cure for Areúsa's *mal de madre* (VII, 203). According to the sixteenth-century *Celestina comentada*, this remedy is derived from Avicenna (Ruggerio 61).

one traditional cure that is far more vulgar and obscene than anything that appears in Rojas's continuation of *Celestina:*

> E final mente si otro consejo no tuuieremos, fagamos el consejo delas viejas: porque ellas la disfamen [a la amada] & la desonesten en quanto pudieren, que ellas tienen arte sagaz para estas cosas mas que los ombres. E dize Auicena que algunos son que se gozan en oyr las cosas fediondas & las que no son licitas. Por ende busque se vna bieja de muy feo acatamiento con grandes dientes & baruas & con fea & vil vestidura: & traya debaxo de si vn paño vntado conel menstruo de la muger. & venga al enamorado & comience a dezir mal de su enamorada: diziendo le que es tiñosa & borracha & que se mea en la cama & que es epilentica: & fiere de pie & de mano: & que es corrompida: & que en su cuerpo tiene torondos, especial mente en su natura: & que le fiede el fuelgo & es suzia: & diga otras muchas fealdades: las quales saben las viejas dezir: & son para ellos mostradas. E si por aquestas fealdades non la quisiere dexar, saque el paño dela sangre de su costumbre de baxo de sy: & muestre gelo subita mente delante su cara: & de le grandes bozes diziendo: "mira que tal es tu amiga commo este paño." E si con todo esso non la quisiere dexar, ya no es omne saluo diablo encarnado enloquecido: & dende adelante, pierdase con su locura. (qtd. in Seniff 16)

While Rojas's work seems to have much in common with previous works on lovesickness, it also anticipates some of the themes developed in later examinations of melancholy. In England, for example, *Celestina* finds an echo not only in Robert Burton's *The Anatomy of Melancholy*, but also in Timothy Bright's *A Treatise of Melancholie* (1580), the first analysis of this subject in English. Like *Celestina*, Bright's work begins with two introductions, a dedicatory to "the Right Worshipful M. Peter Osbourne," and a letter, "To his Melancholicke Friend: M." Bright indicates that M. is really a "supposed fr[i]end," presented so "that the discourse [will be] more familiar" to the reader (v). Nevertheless, as in Rojas's "El autor a un su amigo," the opening letter emphasizes the realistic nature of M.'s "mournful estate" (ix). What is more, Bright reveals that his concern for his friend has left him in the midst of a melancholic depression, although the author's malady is not nearly as serious as the melancholy that affects M.:

> Although deare M. your letter full of heavines, and uncomfortable plaintes, hath in such fort affected me, that (as it faireth with a true harted friend) your affliction draweth me into the fellowship of your mourneful estate. Whereby I am faine to call for such supporte, as reason ministreth to wisemen: and am compelled as it were to put bit into the mouth of my over vehement affection: and give checke as much as my strength serveith unto my passion somewhat in this behalfe unruly. Yet albeit our cases are not equall, in so much as the griefe is not so sensible to me as to your selfe. (ix)

Coincidentally, Bright appears to be as melancholic as Robert Burton, which suggests that his knowledge of the disease would alleviate the writer's illness as much as the reader's. Yet if by some coincidence both Burton and Bright are melancholics who write about the causes and effects of the disease, one may wonder if Rojas—perhaps by an even greater coincidence—shares this melancholic ailment with the two English writers. Although this possibility may appear to be extraordinarily remote, especially considering the lack of information we have on the *bachiller*, a greater understanding of contemporary theories on the melancholic condition could provide an answer to this question.

The few things that we know about Fernando de Rojas and his reasons for writing the continuation of *Celestina* are found at the beginning of "El autor a un su amigo." Rojas writes:

> Suelen los que de sus tierras absentes se fallan considerar de qué cosa aquel lugar donde parten mayor inopia o falta padezca para con la tal servir a los conterráneos, de quien en algún tiempo beneficio recebido tienen; y viendo que legítima obligación a investigar lo semijante me compelía para pagar las muchas mercedes de vuestra libre liberalidad recebidas, asaz vezes retraýdo en mi cámara, acostado sobre mi propia mano, echando mis sentidos por ventores y my juyzio a bolar, me venía a la memoria no sólo la necessidad que nuestra común patria tiene de la presente obra por la muchedumbre de galanes y enamorados mancebos que posee, pero aun en particular vuestra mesma persona. (69)

According to the letter's opening paragraph, Rojas finds himself far from his home in the Puebla de Montalván, but he often thinks about how he could benefit his hometown. We know that the *bachiller* is concerned about the town's *enamorados mancebos* in general and about his friend's lovesick state in particular, but this passage contains one essential detail about Rojas's condition that is not immediately apparent to the modern reader. The *bachiller* describes himself in his room in Salamanca, thinking about home, "asaz vezes retravdo en [su] cámara, acostado sobre [su] propia mano, echando [sus] sentidos por ventores y [su] juyzio a bolar" (69).

To *Celestina*'s modern readers, Rojas may appear to be a typical university student with far too much time on his hands, but in reality this brief self-description strongly suggests that the *bachiller* is also suffering from some of the common symptoms of melancholy. As Ioan P. Couliano has noted, melancholics receive their name because they are dominated by the humor of black bile, or *melaina chole* in Greek. Their temperament corresponds to the element of earth, which is cold and dry. Melancholics are frequently dishonest and prone to anger, yet they are passionate when they fall in love, which explains why *amor hereos* is traditionally identified with this humoral state. Nevertheless, while these personal characteristics are normally associated with cold black bile, Aristotle notes in the "Problems" that, like most liquids, this bodily humor has the capacity to change its temperature (2:1500). In contrast to the standard cold humor, which normally leads to despondency, Couliano notes, there is a second kind of melancholy that produces a totally different effect:

> Theophrastus early differentiates between two kinds of melancholy; this was later reiterated by Aristotle. One kind, produced by cold black bile, answers to the above-mentioned characteristics, whereas the other, caused by the predominance of the *hot* humor, confers upon the subject a psychic liability and instability that goes with genius.... What are these exceptional tendencies of the melancholic [of genius]? ... This brings with it, besides a prodigious memory, an extraordinary capacity for analysis. That is why, Ficino tells us, "all the great men who have ever excelled in an art have been melancholic, either because they were born so or became so through assiduous meditation." (47–48)

According to this description, a hot melancholic would be a man of genius with extraordinary artistic talent. He would exhibit outstanding analytical abilities, perhaps caused by what Ficino calls assiduous meditation. In other words, he could very well be a brilliant writer who—like Rojas—finds himself "asaz vezes retravdo en [su] cámara ...

echando [sus] sentidos por ventores y [su] juyzio a bolar" (69). Nevertheless, while Rojas apparently exhibits some of the typical qualities of the melancholic of genius, there is another important question about the *bachiller's* depiction: why would Rojas portray himself in "El autor a un su amigo" as "acostado sobre [su] propia mano" (69)? The explanation for this apparently insignificant detail appears in Giorgio Agamben's modern description of the medieval melancholic:

> Melancholy or black bile . . . is the humor whose disorders are liable to produce the most destructive consequences. In medieval humoral cosmology, melancholy is traditionally associated with the earth, autumn (or winter), the dry element, cold, the north wind, the color black, old age (or maturity); its planet is Saturn. . . . The physiological symptoms of *abundantia melancholiae* (abundance of melancholy humor) includes darkening of the skin, blood, and urine, hardening of the pulse, burning in the gut, flatulence, acid burping, *whistling in the left ear*, constipation or excess of feces, and gloomy dreams. (11; emphasis added)

Agamben's account of the humoral condition reveals that melancholics hear a whistling sound in the left ear, a physical reaction that matches one of the common symptoms of passionate love found in the Arcipreste de Talavera: "[C]asi el oýr fallesce, que paréscele como que oye abejones en el oreja" (52). More important, Agamben also indicates that the whistling or buzzing sound produced by the illness is directly responsible for the typical gesture of the melancholic: "This symptom . . . perhaps best explains the gesture of holding up the head with the left hand, so characteristic of the depictions of the melancholic temperament (in the oldest representations, the melancholic often appeared standing, in the act of squeezing his left ear with his hand)" (14 n. 2).

It appears from Agamben's explanation that Rojas may describe himself as *acostado sobre [su] propia mano* not out of a sense of sloth or laziness, but perhaps to counter the whistling that melancholics hear in their left ear. Yet irrespective of the precise cause, additional examples of this common gesture appear in works such as *The Anatomy of Melancholy*. The introduction is titled "Democritus Junior to the Reader" because Burton adopts the identity of this classical scholar when he writes *The Anatomy*. In the engraving in the frontispiece, however, Democritus is pictured as a melancholic with his head in his left hand, accompanied by the following opening poem:

> Old Democritus under a tree,
> Sits on a stone with book on knee,
> About him hang there many features,
> Of cats, dogs, and such like creatures,
> Of which he makes anatomy,
> The seat of black choler to see.
> Over his head appears the sky,
> And Saturn Lord of Melancholy. (1:7)

According to Burton's study, hypochondria is one of the most common manifestations of melancholy, along with the characteristic behavior of jealousy, solitariness, and superstition. Like Democritus, the hypochondriac is also pictured in the frontispiece with his face in his left hand, and an accompanying poem that explains his physical ailment:

> *Hypocondriacus* leans on his arm,
> Wind in his side doth him much harm,
> And troubles him full sore, God knows,
> Much pain he hath and many woes.
> About his pottes and glasses lie,
> newly brought from's apothecary,
> This Saturn's aspects signify,
> You see them portray'd in the sky.[8]

The gesture of the hand resting on the head is derived from the physiological symptoms of melancholy, but the European pictorial tradition reveals that this stance is also related to the melancholic's pensive nature. As Klibansky, Panofsky, and Saxl have written, "The primary significance of this age-old gesture . . . is grief, but it may also mean fatigue or creative thought. . . . In medieval portraits of Saturn and melancholy . . . this motif frequently receded into the background, but even then it was never quite forgotten; see, for instance, the description of Saturn in King Alfonso's *Book of Chess* as a sad old man, 'la mano ala mexiella como omne cuyerdadoso'" (286–87).

---

8. In the section titled "Symptomes of Windy Hypocondriacall Melancholy" (I.3.2.2.), Burton notes that "[t]*heir ears sing now and then*, vertigo and giddiness come by fits, turbulent dreams, dryness, leanness" (411; emphasis added), but this symptom is not confined to hypochondriacs. In "Symptoms, or Signs of Melancholy in the Body" (I.3.1.1), Burton indicates that Hippocrates describes melancholics as "leane, withered, hollow-eyed, look old, wrinkled, harsh, much troubled with wind and a griping in their bellies . . . dejected looks, flaggy beards, *singing of the ears*" (383; emphasis added).

The best-known artistic rendition of the melancholic gesture appears in Albrecht Dürer's 1517 engraving *Melencolia I* (see Agamben, fig. 1; Klibansky, Panofsky, and Saxl 1; or Panofsky 209), which shows the female figure of melancholy with her head resting in her left hand. Many other sixteenth-century engravings and paintings of the female figure of melancholy repeat the same motif (Klibansky, figs. 114, 115, 118, 122, 123, 126, 131, 134, and 135).[9] Peter Paul Rubens presents a similar attitude in *Heraclitus as a Melancholie* (Agamben, fig. 3), although the classical scholar is depicted in the painting with his face in his right hand rather than in his left. The typical left-handed pose also appears in Giulio Campagnola's fifteenth-century engraving of Saturn (Klibansky, Panofsky, and Saxl, fig. 54), as well as in Girolamo da Santa Croce's sixteenth-century painting of this mythological god (Klibansky, Panofsky, and Saxl, fig. 56).[10] The same gesture is found in one of the figures in the foreground of Raphael's *The School of Athens* (Dussler, pl. 124), although scholars are uncertain whether the figure is Heraclitus or Michelangelo.

Moreover, John F. Moffit (1978) has noted that the melancholic pose is also used in the traditional representation of Europe's most gifted writers, especially its poets. Commenting on José de Ribera's seventeenth-century print *The Poet* (Brown 91), Moffit writes:

> A full-length figure rests ponderously against a time-worn squared masonry block. "The Poet" bends his left arm which supports his head. His face is in shadow and the brow furrowed in deep thought. . . . The general nature of his profession may be easily corroborated from the complementary combination of two traditional attributes. On the one hand, the laurel wreath, the adornment of *homo literatus*, is denotative of a "victory" in the liberal arts. On the other, the very attitude of the figure—with pensive head resting on hand and downcast and closed

---

9. The melancholic pose is also used in the pictorial rendering of saints, such as in Antonio Pereda's and Mateo Cerezo's paintings of Saint Jerome (Brown 46 and 47), both of which are reminiscent of José de Ribera's *The Poet* (Brown 44).

10. Panofsky writes: "Once established, this 'consonance' between melancholy and Saturn was never questioned. Every human being, mineral, plant, or animal supposed to have a melancholy nature—among them, for instance, the dog and the bat—*ipso facto* 'belonged' to Saturn, too. The very posture of sadness, with the head resting on the hand, is melancholy as well as Saturnian; and as the black gall was considered the most ignoble of humors, so the 'Saturnus impius' held to be the most unfortunate of celestial influences" (166). See also Klibansky, Panofsky, and Saxl 1964, part II, "Saturn, the Star of Melancholy," 125–214.

eyes—is indicative of the traditional concept of "poetic melancholy." (75-76)

In light of this literary and artistic tradition, Rojas's physical and mental state in "El autor a un su amigo" suggests that the *bachiller* is the typical melancholic of genius. This humoral condition would explain not only why Rojas prepares such a masterful continuation of *Celestina*, but also why he stresses the "lid y offensión" that characterizes the natural world as well as all human activity (77). The surprisingly pessimistic prologue, which may strike the reader as a discordant element in the work, seems to be the result of Rojas's saturnine condition. This morose quality further reinforces the credibility of the text's instructional message because—as a melancholic of genius—the *bachiller* would find it natural to stress *Celestina*'s profound instructional values rather than its more superficial lascivious qualities.

Moreover, while the author's melancholy helps to explain the despondent message of the prologue, it may also clarify the essence of Pleberio's lament in Act XXI. Although the father's *planctus* has a vital place in the text, appearing at the very conclusion of *Celestina*, modern scholars do not agree about its true meaning or its precise connection with the rest of the work.[11] Nevertheless, as Stephen Gilman (1972) has noted, the relationship between Rojas and Pleberio appears to be significant because the old man's soliloquy

> occupies a final act all to itself; it serves as a concluding monologue after all the participants in the dialogue have died or disappeared; it emerges from the soul of the one character who has not been undermined ironically during the course of the work; and above all it sums up and attempts to make sense—or nonsense—of all that has taken place. In view of these self-evident facts ... it requires a suspicious amount of critical dexterity to avoid attributing to the young author the words of the aged character. As Menéndez Pelayo affirmed explicitly (and as almost all other readers before or since have assumed tacitly) Pleberio in Act XXI is the spokesman for Rojas's final intention, the intention as redefined in the course of writing *La Celestina*. (360)

11. There is an extensive bibliography on Pleberio's lament. See for example Lida de Malkiel 471–88; Wardropper 1964; Fraker 1966; Dunn 1976; Gerli; Shipley 1985; Vicente; Severin 1989, 105–15; Deyermond 1990; and Snow.

In contrast to Gilman's confident assertions about the significance of Pleberio's lament, most scholars do not agree that the old man is the mouthpiece for Rojas's authorial intentions. Alan Deyermond (1990), for example, writes:

> Pleberio's lament for Melibea, which occupies virtually all of *Celestina*'s last act, invites the scrutiny of readers who, in the absence of third-person authorial guidance within the text of this enigmatic novel-in-dialogue, hope to find a trustworthy spokesman for the author. Their hopes are not fulfilled. Although Marcel Bataillon's reasons for rejecting Pleberio as the author's mouthpiece have not inspired general agreement, the critical consensus now accepts his conclusion: "En se réservant le dernier mot pour 'tirer la morale,' l'auteur Rojas confirme notre impression que Pleberio, *paterfamilias ex machina* dont la déploration final exprime le désespoir impuissant devant la catastrophe, est un personnage trop terne, un trop mauvais représentant de la fonction paternelle, pour tirer la leçon de ce drame en marge duquel il este demeuré sans en rien savoir" [218]. (169)[12]

Although Gilman and Deyermond take diametrically opposing positions on whether Pleberio serves as the spokesman for Fernando de Rojas, the differences between these two critical stances may not be as great as they appear to be. Gilman writes that it would take "critical

---

12. Deyermond perhaps undermines his own argument by denying, then affirming, the Christian background of Pleberio's lament. Deyermond first observes: "Perhaps the most important reason in favour of Bataillon's view ... is the incompatibility between Pleberio's attitude and that of Fernando de Rojas as set out in the prefatory and valedictory material in prose and verse. The two prologues, and the poems at the beginning and the end of the work, give a firmly Christian interpretation, and that there is good reason to think that even if in the [*Comedia*] ... the authorial Christian morality is fairly conventional ... it has become a deeply-felt personal commitment by the time Rojas revises his work as the ... *Tragicomedia*.... Yet Pleberio seems to feel no concern for the fate of his beloved daughter's soul" (170).

After denying the spiritual content of Pleberio's lament, Deyermond later repeats Peter Dunn's observation that the *planctus* ends with a quote from a Catholic hymn, which in turn is derived from the Psalms: "The religious origin of the other part of the frame [Act XXI] is obvious; when Pleberio ends his speech with the despairing cry '¿Por qué me dexaste triste y solo in hac lachrymarum valle?' he is quoting directly from a hymn, *Salve regina*" (Deyermond 177-78). More important, Deyermond ignores the fact that Pleberio's lament specifically indicates that love's fire indeed consumes the human soul: "Tu fuego es ardiente rayo que jamás haze señal do llega. La leña que gasta tu llama son almas y vidas de humanas criaturas" (XXI, 342).

dexterity" to ignore the relationship between author and character; Deyermond notes that readers "hope to find a trustworthy spokesman for the author," but this expectation is not realized. Both scholars thus agree that there should be a definite connection between Rojas and Pleberio, although they disagree about whether it exists. In addition, while most scholars would reject Gilman's stance that Pleberio and Rojas adopt a neo-Stoic attitude derived from the *bachiller's converso* pessimism, many would conclude that a connection of some sort is expected.

The resolution of these two contradictory readings may lie in discovering a reasonable, verifiable nexus between the opening letter and prologue on the one hand, and Act XXI on the other, a connection that is perhaps found in the melancholy that permeates both sections of *Celestina*. According to Charles F. Fraker's study of the humoral condition of *Celestina's* characters (1993), Pleberio is possibly melancholic, but he is almost certainly saturnine. As mentioned above (this chapter, n. 11), medieval scholars believed that there was a special relationship between Saturn and melancholy, so Fraker's observation directly links Pleberio to a possible melancholic state. Fraker writes:

> Klibanksy and his collaborators quote some lines about melancholy Saturn from an influential Arabic text, by Alcabitius, available in Latin and well-known in Christian Europe . . . [that indicates that] Saturn rules over different kinds and classes of people. The author distinguishes clearly between good influences and bad. On its good side the planet has power over "fathers . . . over old age and dotage and over elder brothers and ancestors, and over honesty in speech and in love, and absence of impulses . . . , and over experience of things . . . ; he presides over lasting, permanent things, like land, husbandry, farming, tilling the land, and over respectable professions which have to do with water like the commanding of ships and their management, and the administration of work" [131]. The . . . relevance to *Celestina's* presentation of the honorable and enterprising Pleberio is obvious. The allusion here to ships is striking; a coincidence, perhaps we recall the "navíos" in the old man's last speech [XXI, 337]. (144–45)

While these personal characteristics associate Pleberio with a possible saturnine condition, his lament also appears to contain specific melancholic attributes. The *planctus* reveals that Pleberio's youth was affected by the *brasas* of love's fires (XXI, 341), which implies that the old man suffered from erotic melancholy in his younger days. More important, his "triste experiencia" (XXI, 338) over sixty years has soured him on all mundane concerns, and has made him lose faith in any sense of worldly order. It therefore appears that over time—perhaps as a result of the assiduous contemplation described by Marsilio Ficino—Pleberio has become a man of learning who shares the same pessimistic stance on life that characterizes Fernando de Rojas's melancholia:

> Yo pensava en mi más tierna edad que eras y eran tus hechos regidos por alguna orden. Agora, visto el pro y la contra de tus bienandanças, me pareçes un laberinto de errores, un desierto spantable, una morada de fieras, juego de hombres que andan en corro, laguna llena de cieno, región llena de spinas, monte alto, campo pedregoso, prado lleno de serpientes, huerto florido y sin fruto, fuente de cuydados, río de lágrimas, mar de miserias, trabajo sin provecho, dulce ponçoña, vana esperança, falsa alegría, verdadero dolor. (XXI, 338)

Since Rojas and Pleberio share a similar incurable pessimism, it is unsurprising that both of them use the same author as the principal source for the prologue and the *planctus*. As Alan Deyermond (1975) has demonstrated, Rojas briefly and carelessly cites Petrarca in the prologue, but "this cavalier treatment of borrowed material does not disguise the fact that all the first half of the *Prólogo* is Petrarchan, to a greater extent, and with less originality, than any other part of *La Celestina*" (52). Deyermond explains that the prologue's "batalla" (77), "lid y offensión" (77), and "guerra" (78) come directly from Petrarca (Deyermond 54), but significantly so does all of the conflictive material quoted above from Pleberio's lament (Deyermond 73).

Even though Pleberio's wisdom allows him to see the continual strife that characterizes all human existence, like Rojas the old man realizes that this earthly disorder is not always evident. Pleberio describes an inherently deceptive world that offers the illusory attraction of mundane pleasures, while it simultaneously prepares a catastrophic surprise for those who are foolish enough to be drawn in by these earthly delights: "Cévanos, mundo falso, con el manjar de tus deleytes; al mejor sabor descubres el anzuelo; no lo podemos huyr, que nos tiene ya caçadas las voluntades . . . Corremos por los prados de tus viciosos vicios muy descuydados . . . ; descúbrenos la celada quando ya no ay lugar de bolver" (XXI, 338–39).

Rojas's prologue suggests that all earthly activity is a battle or war, but Pleberio develops this idea further in Act XXI by including material pleasures as an integral part of the world's destructive chaos. Expanding on Rojas's use of martial expressions, the old man indicates that the false world hunts down its human prey, as it lies in ambush of its unwitting victims and attacks them when it is too late for them to save themselves. Pleberio's *planctus* thus works within the general parameters of struggle and disorder established by the author in the prefatory material, but he also uses this conceptual framework to underline the human tragedy of mundane desires.

More important, Pleberio's lament reveals that worldly vices can fool us with "el manjar de [s]us deleytes" (XXI, 339), a concept that suggests that Rojas may have decided to fight back against sensual pleasures on their own terms. As noted above, Rojas writes in the acrostic verses from "El autor a un su amigo" that when a sick person cannot swallow a "píldora amarga," then the solution is to "mete[r]la dentro del dulce manjar" (73). The author's *manjar* in *Celestina* is precisely its lascivious activity—the same *manjar* that the world offers us—but with a radically different intention. Instead of condemning us to eternal damnation as authentic sensual pleasures do, Rojas's *manjar* demonstrates the perils of earthly delights so that wise readers "escarmientan y arrojan su carga" rather than remain subject to their poisonous influence (73).

Although most modern scholars may not see any verifiable relationship between Rojas and Pleberio, the confluence of sources, ideas, and themes found in the introductory material and Act XXI repeatedly reinforces the correlation between author and character. Nevertheless, the final confirmation of this nexus occurs when the old man denounces love as the principal cause of the earthly disorder that surrounds him. As we have seen, the prefatory and valedictory material in the *Auto*, the *Comedia*, and the *Tragicomedia* repeatedly censures the *desordenado apetito* of lovesickness (82), but Pleberio's lament takes this reprimand even further by noting that love's power is far greater than he ever imagined.[13] The old man was always aware of the many

---

13. Charles F. Fraker (1966) writes: "The *World* is, with the flesh and the devil, one of the three enemies of the soul, something the Christian should put no trust in. Rojas identifies Pleberio's pessimism with what might be called Christian pessimism. Once again, the charge of conscious infidelity on Rojas's part, if Pleberio is really his mouthpiece, is hard to maintain. The views put forth in *Celestina* might not have been to the liking of every theologian, but they lie well within the range of a less formal sort of orthodoxy. We must now ask ourselves whether the world view we have outlined is really Rojas' own or, what is more to the point, whether it has any bearing on the thematic substance of the *Celestina*. The strongest piece of evidence to the affirmative comes to light as we study the ways the authors of the *Celestina* conceived its chief matter, love. It is

dangers inherent in love's *lazos*, but he never expected that they could still lead to death and destruction so many years after liberating himself from their devastating passions: "¡O amor, amor, que no pensé que tenías fuerça ni poder de matar a tus sujectos! . . . No pensé que tomavas en los hijos la vengança de los padres, ni sé si hieres con hierro, ni si quemas con huego; sana dexas la ropa; lastimas el coraçón. Hazes que feo amen y hermoso les paresca. ¿Quién te dio tanto poder?" (XXI, 341).

By the end of Act XXI, there is little for Pleberio to do but mourn the great personal loss that is caused by love's destructive nature. Pleberio—much like Ficino, Castiglione, and other Renaissance writers—recognizes that amorous desire is the "[e]nemigo de toda razón" (XXI, 342), which means that it destroys the human faculty that traditionally has guided mankind toward virtue and salvation. Moreover, lovesickness suppresses the contemplative nature that is the defining characteristic of the melancholic of genius. Without this spiritual direction, the inevitable result of human sensuality is the devastation of the immortal soul, regardless of one's beliefs or religion: "Ciego te pintan, [Amor,] pobre y moço. . . . La leña que gasta tu llama son almas y vidas de humanas criaturas, las quales son tantas que de quién començar pueda apenas me ocurre; no sólo de christianos mas de gentiles y judíos y todo en pago de buenos servicios" (XXI, 342).

Following a long Greek, Latin, Arabic, and vernacular tradition, Pleberio determines that love is directly responsible for both Melibea's suicide and his present suffering. Love created Melibea, but it also drove her to her death; it established the deep emotional ties between father and daughter, but it now produces his unspeakable agony: "[N]o nascida [Melibea], no amara; no amando, cessara mi quexosa y desconsolada postremería" (XXI, 343). Viewing his disastrous circumstances, Pleberio concludes that there is no possible solution for his present suffering. The old man faces an overwhelming tragedy that has left him anguished, alone, and forsaken in this vale of tears, and his final words to his departed daughter reveal that there is no solace to be found in his moment of greatest need: "Por qué te mostraste tan cruel con tu viejo padre? ¿Por qué me dexaste, quando yo te havía de dexar? ¿Por qué

---

plainly asserted at various points in the work that love is a violation of universal harmony. Love as a source of *disorder* is certainly the burden of a large segment of Pleberio's soliloquy" (520). See also Fraker's astute analysis of the disorder and chaos produced by mundane love (524–26), and of the relationship between Rojas and Pleberio (529).

Significantly, Rojas's acrostic verses also link Pleberio's lament with the *antiguo auctor*'s opening argument: "Si bien discernéys mi limpio motivo . . . / buscad bien el fin de aquesto que escrivo / o del principio leed su argumento" (72–73).

me dexaste penado? ¿Por qué me dexaste triste y solo *hac lacrimarum valle?*" (XXI, 343).

The commonality of ideas that exists in the opening letter, the prologue, Act XXI, and *Celestina*'s closing verses creates a textual framework that encloses the dramatic action of the first fifteen acts of the *Comedia*, and later the first twenty acts of the *Tragicomedia*. This philosophical structure—resulting from the melancholic and tragic attitude toward life on the part of both the young author and the aged character—serves as a beginning and closing commentary on *Celestina* that not only emphasizes the text's didactic purpose, but also joins the work to a centuries-old tradition that condemns the catastrophic consequences of passionate love. As noted in the preceding chapters of this study, medieval and Renaissance writers continually bemoan the tragic results of *amor hereos*, especially among the *mancebos* who were most vulnerable to the illness. Although many critics believe that Rojas and Pleberio have little in common, in reality both author and character frame *Celestina* within a common philosophical setting that emphasizes the importance of the work's instructional message.

By concentrating on the story's development rather than on its fundamental didactic purpose, modern scholars have become like the readers that Fernando de Rojas criticizes for turning the work into a "cuento de camino" (80). Although this approach to *Celestina* violates the author's stated didactic purpose, we know from Keith Whinnom's research on the Golden Age bestseller (1980) that it is difficult to understand fully the era's cultural and literary standards, not to mention the "heavy emphasis on moral lessons" found in so many works in that period (195). Although our critical commentary of Golden Age texts cannot provide a faithful recreation of contemporary approaches to literature, if we are to appreciate the extent of *Celestina*'s achievement—not to mention its importance in Spanish Renaissance culture—then we must recognize the historical conditions in which it was created, as well as the principal author's description of the informed reader: "Pero aquellos para cuyo verdadero plazer es todo, desechan el cuento de la hystoria para contar, coligen la suma para su provecho, ríen lo donoso, las sentencias y dichos de philósophos guardan en su memoria para trasponer en lugares convenibles a sus autos y propósitos" (80).

Works Cited

Abélard and Héloïse. N.d. *Lettres complètes d'Abélard et d'Héloïse*. Translated by M. Gréard. Paris: Garnier Frères.
———. 1974. *The Letters of Abelard and Heloise*. Translated by Betty Radice. London: Penguin Books.
Achilles Tatius. 1917. *Clitophon and Leucippe*. Translated by S. Gaselle. London: William Heineman.
Agamben, Giorgio. 1993. *Stanzas: Word and Phantasm in Western Culture*. Translated by Ronald L. Martínez. Minneapolis: University of Minnesota Press.
Aristotle. 1984. *The Complete Works of Aristotle*. Edited by Jonathan Barnes. 2 vols. Princeton: Princeton University Press.
Armas, Frederick A. de. 1975. "*La Celestina*: An Example of Love Melancholy." *Romanic Review* 46:288–95.
———. 1994. "Black Sun: Woman, Saturn, and Melancholia in Claramonte's *La estrella de Sevilla*." *Journal of Interdisciplinary Literary Studies* 6:19–36.
Asensio, Manuel. 1952. "El tiempo en *La Celestina*." *Hispanic Review* 20:28–43.
———. 1953. "A Rejoinder [to Stephen Gilman]." *Hispanic Review* 21:45–50.
Augustine. 1982. *The Literal Meaning of Genesis*. Edited and translated by John Hammond Taylor. 2 vols. New York: Newman Press.
———. 1991. *Two Books on Genesis Against the Manichees. On Genesis*. Edited and translated by Roland J. Teske. Washington, D.C.: Catholic University of America Press.
Avicenna. 1945. *A Treatise on Love by Ibn Sina*. Translated by Emil L. Fackenheim. *Medieval Studies* 7:208–28.
Babb, Lawrence. 1965. *The Elizabethan Malady: A Study of Melancholia in English Literature from 1580 to 1642*. East Lansing: Michigan State University Press, 1951. Reprint.
Bataillon, Marcel. 1961. *La Célestine selon Fernando de Rojas*. Paris: Didier.
———. 1967. *Défense et illustration du sens littéral*. London: Modern Humanities Research Association.

Beardsley, Theodore S. 1993. "Kaspar von Barth's Neo-Latin Translation of *Celestina*." In *Fernando de Rojas and* Celestina: *Approaching the Fifth Centenary*, edited by Ivy A. Corfis and Joseph T. Snow, 237-50. Madison, Wis.: Hispanic Seminary of Medieval Studies.

Boccaccio, Giovanni. 1939. *L'elegia di Madonna Fiammetta*. Bari: Giuseppi Laterza & Figli.

———. 1986. *Amorosa visione: Bilingual Edition*. Edited and translated by Robert Hollander, Timothy Hampton, and Margherita Frankel. Hanover: University Press of New England.

———. 1990. *The Elegy of Lady Fiammetta*. Edited and translated by Mariangela Causa-Steindler and Thomas Mauch. Chicago: University of Chicago Press.

Bodenham, C. H. L. 1985. "The Nature of the Dream in Late Mediaeval French Literature." *Medium Ævum* 54:74–86.

Bright, Timothy. 1940. *A Treatise of Melancholie*. Edited by Hardin Craig. New York: Columbia University Press.

Brown, Jonothan. 1973. *Jusepe de Ribera: Prints and Drawings*. Princeton: Princeton University Press.

Burton, Robert. 1964. *The Anatomy of Melancholy*. 3 vols. London: Dent Everyman's Library.

Cantarino, Vicente. 1977. "Didactismo y moralidad de *La Celestina*." In *La Celestina y su contorno social. Actas del I Congreso Internacional sobre La Celestina*. Edited by Manuel Criado del Val. Barcelona: Borrás.

Capellanus, Andreas. 1982. *Andreas Capellanus on Love*. Translated by P. G. Walsh. London: Duckworth.

Cárdenas, Anthony J. 1988. "The *Conplisiones de los onbres* of the *Arcipreste de Talavera* and the Male Lovers of the *Celestina*." *Hispania* 71:479-91.

Castells, Ricardo. 1990. "El sueño de Calisto y la tradición celestinesca." *Celestinesca* 14 (1): 17–39.

———. 1991. "Calisto and the Imputed Parody of Courtly Love in *Celestina*." *Journal of Hispanic Philology* 15:209–20.

———. 1993a. "El mal de amores de Calisto y el diagnóstico de Eras y Crato, médicos." *Hispania* 76:55–60.

———. 1993b. "On the *cuerpo glorificado* and the *visión divina*." *Romance Notes* 34:97–100.

———. 1995. *Calisto's Dream and the Celestinesque Tradition: A Rereading of* Celestina. Carolina Studies in the Romance Languages and Literatures. Chapel Hill: University of North Carolina Press.

Castiglione, Baldassare. 1967. *The Book of the Courtier. From the Italian of Count Baldassare Castiglione: Done into English by Sir Thomas Hoby, Anno 1561*. Edited by Walter Raleigh. London: David Nutt, 1900. Reprint, New York: AMS Press.

———. 1972. *Il libro del Cortegiano*. Edited by Ettore Bonora. Milan: Grande Universale Mursia.

Castro, Adolfo de. 1950. "Apuntes biográficos [sobre Villalobos]." Madrid: Atlas BAE 36, xi–xxiv.

Celsus. 1960. *De Medicina*. Translated by W. G. Spencer. 3 vols. Cambridge: Harvard University Press.

Cervantes, Miguel de. 1998. *Don Quijote de la Mancha*. Edited by Francisco Rico. Barcelona: Instituto Cervantes.

Chrétien de Troyes. 1994. *Cligés. Romans suivis des Chansons, avec, en appendice, Philomena*. Edited and translated by C. Méla and O. Collet, 285–494. Paris: La Pochotèque.

———. 1997. *Cligès*. Translated by Burton Raffel. New Haven: Yale University Press.

Ciavolella, Massimo. 1986. "Eros/Ereos: Marsilio Ficino's Interpretation of Guido Cavalcanti's 'Donna me prega.'" In *Ficino and Renaissance Neoplatonism*, edited by Konrad Eisenbichler and Olga Zorzi Pugliese, 39–48. Toronto: Dovehouse.

Couliano, Ioan P. 1987. *Eros and Magic in the Renaissance*. Translated by Margaret Cook. Chicago: University of Chicago Press.

Dante Alighieri. 1995. *Vita nuova: Italian Text with Facing English Translation*. Vol. 1. Edited and translated by Dino S. Cervigni and Edward Vasta. Notre Dame: University of Notre Dame Press.

"De Guillaume au faucon." 1982. In *Cuckolds, Clerics, and Countrymen: Medieval French Fabliaux*, edited by Raymond Eichman, translated by John DuVal, 87–104. Fayetteville: University of Arkansas Press.

Deyermond, Alan. 1961. "The Text-Book Mishandled: Andreas Capellanus and the Opening Scene of *La Celestina*." *Neophilologus* 45:218–21.

———. 1975. *The Petrarchan Sources of* La Celestina. Oxford: Clarendon Press, 1961. Reprint, Westport, Conn.: Greenwood Press.

———. 1990. "Pleberio's Lost Investment: The Worldly Perspective of *Celestina*, Act 21." *MLN* 105:169–79.

———. 1991. Introduction to "The *argumento* of *Celestina*," by Keith Whinnom. *Celestinesca* 15 (1): 19–21.

Dulaey, Martine. 1973. *La rêve dans la vie et la pensée de Saint Augustin*. Paris: Études Augustiniennes.

Dunn, Peter N. 1975. *Fernando de Rojas*. Boston: Twayne.

———. 1976. "Pleberio's World." *PMLA* 91:406–19.

Dussler, Luitpold. 1970. *Raphael: A Critical Catalogue of His Pictures, Wall-Paintings, and Tapestries*. Translated by Sebastian Cruff. New York: Phaidon.

Faulhaber, Charles B. 1990. "*Celestina* de Palacio: Madrid, Biblioteca de Palacio, MS 1520." *Celestinesca* 14 (2): 3–39.

———. 1991. "*Celestina* de Palacio: Rojas's Holograph Manuscript." *Celestinesca* 15 (1): 3–52.

Ferrand, Jacques. N.d. *Erotomania, or a Treatise Discoursing of the Essence, Causes, Symptomes, Prognosticks, and Cure of Love or Erotique Melancholy*. Oxford: L. Lichtfield, 1640. Reprint, Ann Arbor, Mich.: University Microfilms.

Ficino, Marsilio. 1944. *Marsilio Ficino's Commentary of Plato's Symposium*. Edited and translated by Sears Reynolds Jayne. University of Missouri Studies. Columbia: University of Missouri Press.

Fox, Ruth A. 1976. *The Tangled Chain: The Structure of Disorder in* The Anatomy of Melancholy. Berkeley and Los Angeles: University of California Press.
Fraker, Charles F. 1966 "The Importance of Pleberio's Soliloquy." *Romanische Forschungen* 78:515–29.
———. 1993. "The Four Humors in Celestina." In *Fernando de Rojas and Celestina: Approaching the Fifth Centenary,* edited by Ivy A. Corfis and Joseph T. Snow, 129–54. Madison: Hispanic Seminary of Medieval Studies.
García, Michel. "1994. Consideraciones sobre *Celestina* de Palacio." *Celestinesca* 18 (1): 3–16.
García Ballester, Luis. 1984. *Los moriscos en la medicina.* Madrid: Labor Universitaria.
Garci-Gómez, Miguel. 1982. "Eros y crato médicos: identificación e interpretación." *Celestinesca* 6 (1): 9–14.
———. 1985. "El sueño de Calisto." *Celestinesca* 9 (1): 11–22.
———. 1986. "*Eras e Crato médicos*: identificación e interpretación." *Celestinesca* 6 (1): 9–14.
———. 1994. *Calisto, soñador y altanero.* Kassel: Edition Reichenberger.
Gerli, E. Michael. 1976. "Pleberio's Lament and Two Literary *Topoi: Expositor* and *Planctus.*" *Romanische Forschungen* 88:67–74.
Gilman, Stephen. 1945. "El tiempo y el género literario en *La Celestina.*" *Revista de Filología Hispánica* 7:147–59.
———. 1953. "A Propos of 'El tiempo en *La Celestina*' by Manuel Asensio." *HR* 21:42–45.
———. 1956. *The Art of* La Celestina. Madison: University of Wisconsin Press.
———. 1972. *The Spain of Fernando de Rojas.* Princeton: Princeton University Press.
Green, Otis H. 1963–66. *Spain and the Western Tradition: The Castilian Mind in Literature from* El Cid *to Calderón.*" 4 vols. Madison: University of Wisconsin Press.
———. 1965. "The Artistic Originality of *La Celestina.*" *Hispanic Review* 33:15–31.
Harrison, Robert Pogue. 1988. *The Body of Beatrice.* Baltimore: Johns Hopkins University Press.
Hippocrates. 1967. *Heracleitus on the Universe.* Edited and translated by W. H. S. Jones. London: William Heinemann.
Jackson, Stanley W. 1986. *Melancholia and Depression: From Hippocratic Times to Modern Times.* New Haven: Yale University Press..
Jacquart, Danielle. 1991. *La medicina árabe y Occidente. Toledo, siglos XII–XIII. Musulmanes, cristianos y judíos: la sabiduría y la tolerancia.* Edited by Louis Cardaillac. Translated by José Luis Arántegui. Madrid: Alianza.
Kassier, Theodore L. 1976. "*Cancionero* poetry and the *Celestina*: From Metaphor to Reality." *Hispanófila* 56:1–28.
Klibansky, Raymond, Erwin Panofsky, and Fritz Saxl. 1964. *Saturn and Melancholy: Studies in the History of Natural Philosophy, Religion, and Art.* New York: Basic Books.

Kristeller, P. O. 1943. *The Philosophy of Marsilio Ficino*. New York: Columbia University Press.
Kruger, Steven F. 1992. *Dreaming in the Middle Ages*. Cambridge: Cambridge University Press.
Lacarra, María Eugenia. 1989. "La parodia de la ficción sentimental en la Celestina." *Celestinesca* 13 (1): 11–29.
Laurentius, M. Andreas. 1938. *A Discourse of the Preservation of the Sight: of Melancholike Diseases; of Rheumes, and of Old Age*. Translated by Richard Surphlet. Oxford: Shakespeare Society.
Lida de Malkiel, María Rosa. 1970. *La originalidad artística de* La Celestina. Buenos Aires: EUDEBA, 1962. Reprint.
Lowes, John L. 1914. "The Loveres Maladye of Hereos." *Modern Philology* 11:491–546.
Macrobius. 1990. *Commentary of the Dream of Scipio*. Edited and translated by William Harris Stahl. New York: Columbia University Press.
Madrigal del Tostado, Alfonso de. 1892. *Tratado que hizo el Tostado de cómo al ome es necesario amar. Opúsculos literarios de los siglos XIV a XVI*. Edited by Antonio Paz y Meliá, 219–44. Madrid: La Sociedad de Bibliófilos Españoles.
Maravall, José Antonio. 1964. *El mundo social de* La Celestina. Madrid: Gredos.
Marcel, Raymond. 1958. *Marsile Ficin*. Paris: Les Belles Lettres.
Marciales, Miguel. 1985. *Celestina: Tragicomedia de Calisto y Melibea*. Edited by Brian Dutton and Joseph T. Snow. 2 vols. Urbana: University of Illinois Press.
Martin, June Hall. 1972. *Love's Fools: Aucassin, Troilus, Calisto, and the Parody of the Courtly Lover*. London: Tamesis.
Martínez de Toledo, Alfonso. 1970. *Arcipreste de Talavera o Corbacho*. Edited by J. González Muela. Madrid: Castalia.
Martorell, Joanot. 1990. *Tirant lo Blanc i altres escrits*. Edited by Martí de Riquer. Barcelona: Clàssics Catalans Ariel
Martorell, Joanot and Martí Joan de Galba. 1984. *Tirant lo Blanc*. Translated by David H. Rosenthal. New York: Shocken Books.
Maurer, Christopher. 1990. "'Soñé que te . . . dirélo?': el soneto del sueño erótico en los siglos XVI y XVII." *Edad de Oro* 9:149–67.
McGrady, Donald. 1994. "Two Studies on the Text of the *Celestina*." *Romance Philology* 48 (1): 1–21.
McVaugh, Michael R. 1985. Introduction to *Opera Medica Omnia*, by Arnaldi de Villanova, 1:11–39. 3 vols. Barcelona: Seminarum Historiae Medicae Cantabricense.
Medici, Lorenzo de'. 1995. *The Autobiography of Lorenzo de' Medici The Magnificent: A Commentary on My Sonnets*. Edited and translated by James Wyatt Cook. Medieval and Renaissance Texts and Studies. Binghamton: State University of New York Press.
Menéndez Pelayo, Marcelino. 1979. *La Celestina*. Madrid: Austral.
Menéndez Pidal, Ramón. 1917. *Antología de prosistas castellanos*. Madrid: Publicaciones de la Revista de Filología Española.

Michael, Ian. 1991. "*La Celestina* de Palacio: el redescubrimiento del MS. II-1520 (sign. ant. 2.A.4) y su procedencia segoviana." *Revista de Literatura Medieval* 3:149–61.
Moffit, John F. 1978, March. "Observations on the 'Poet' by Ribera." *Paragone* 337:75–90.
———. 1988. "Painters 'Born Under Saturn': The Physiological Explanation." *Art History* 2:195–216.
O'Connell, Michael. 1986. *Robert Burton*. Boston: Twayne.
Orduna, Germán. 1988. *Auto, Comedia, Tragicomedia, Celestina*: Perspectivas críticas de un proceso de creación y recepción literaria. *Celestinesca* 12 (1): 3–8.
Palley, Julian. 1983. *The Ambiguous Mirror: Dreams in Spanish Literature*. Valencia and Chapel Hill: Albatross Hispanófila Ediciones.
Panofsky, Erwin. 1955. *The Life of Albrecht Dürer*. Princeton: Princeton University Press.
Parker, A. A. 1985. *The Philosophy of Love in Spanish Literature, 1480–1680*. Edinburgh: Edinburgh University Press.
Peden, Alison M. 1985. "Macrobius and Medieval Dream Literature." *Medium Ævum* 54:59–73.
Petrarca, Francesco. 1996. *The Canzoniere or Rerum vulgarium fragmenta*. Edited and translated by Mark Musa. Bloomington: Indiana University Press.
Plato. 1978. *The Republic*. Translated by C. M. A. Grube. Indianapolis: Hackett.
———. 1998. *Phaedrus*. Translated by James H. Nichols. Ithaca: Cornell University Press.
Real Academia Española. 1992. *Diccionario de la lengua española*. 2 vols. Madrid: Espasa-Calpe.
Rhazes. 1950. *The Spiritual Physick of Rhazes*. Edited and translated by Arthur J. Arberry. London: John Murray.
Riquer, Martín de. 1957. "Fernando de Rojas y *La Celestina*." *Revista de Filología Española* 41:373–95.
Rojas, Fernando de. 1965. *Tragicomedia de Calixto y Melibea*. Edited by M. Criado del Val and G. D. Trotter. Madrid: CSIC.
———. 1968. *La Celestina*. Edited by Julio Cejador y Frauca. 2 vols. Madrid: Espasa-Calpe.
———. 1987. *La Celestina*. Edited by Dorothy S. Severin. Madrid: Cátedra.
———. 1991. *Comedia o Tragicomedia de Calisto y Melibea*. Edited by Peter E. Russell. Madrid: Castalia.
Ruggerio, M. J. 1970. "*La Celestina*: Didacticism Once More." *Romanische Forschungen* 82:56–64.
Ruiz Ramón, Francisco. 1974. "Nota sobre la autoría del Acto I de *La Celestina*." *Hispanic Review* 42:431–35.
Rumeau, A. 1966. "Introduction à Célestina: 'una cosa bien escusada...'" *Les Langues Neo-latines* LX, 176:1–26.
Seniff, Dennis P. 1986. "Bernardo de Gordonio's *Lilio de Medicina*: A Possible Source of *Celestina*?" *Celestinesca* 10 (1): 13–18.

Severin, Dorothy Sherman. 1970. *Memory in* La Celestina. London: Tamesis Books.

———. 1987. Introduction to *La Celestina*, by Fernando de Rojas, edited by Dorothy S. Severin, 11–64. Madrid: Cátedra..

———. 1989. *Tragicomedy and Novelistic Discourse in* Celestina. Cambridge: Cambridge University Press.

Shipley, George A. 1975. "Concerting Through Conceit: Unconventional Uses of Conventional Sickness Images in *La Celestina*." *Modern Language Review* 70:324–32.

———. 1985. "Authority and Experience in *La Celestina*." *Bulletin of Hispanic Studies* 62:95–111.

Silvestre, Hubert. 1963. "Note sur la survie de Macrobe au Moyen Age." *Classica et Mediaevalia* 24:170–80.

Snow, Joseph. 1990. "Celestina and Pleberio: When Value Systems Collide." *Fifteenth-Century Studies* 17:381–93.

Solomon, Michael. 1989. "Calisto's Ailment: Bitextual Diagnostics and Parody in *Celestina*." *Revista de Estudios Hispánicos* 23:41–64.

———. 1997. *The Literature of Misogyny in Medieval Spain: The* Arcipreste de Talavera *and the* Spill. Cambridge: Cambridge University Press.

Soufas, Teresa S. 1987. "Religious Melancholy and Tirso's Despairing Monk in *El condenado por desconfiado*." *Romance Quarterly* 34:179–88.

———. 1990. *Melancholy and the Secular Mind in Spanish Golden Age Literature*. Columbia: University of Missouri Press.

Stahl, William Harris. Introduction to *Commentary on the Dream of Scipio*, by Macrobius, 3–65. New York: Columbia University Press.

Stamm, James R. 1988. *La estructura de* La Celestina. Salamanca: Ediciones de la Universidad de Salamanca.

Sullerot, Evelyne. 1979. *Women in Love: Eight Centuries of Feminine Writing*. Translated by Helen R. Lane. Garden City, N.Y.: Doubleday.

Truesdell, W. D. 1973. "The Hortus Conclusus Tradition, and the Implications of Its Absence in the *Celestina*." *Kentucky Romance Quarterly* 20:257–77.

Vega, Garcilaso de la. 1974. *Obras completas con comentario*. Edited by Elias L. Rivers. Columbus: Ohio State University Press.

Vicari, Patricia. 1989. *The View from Minerva's Tower: Learning and Imagination in* The Anatomy of Melancholy. Toronto: University of Toronto Press.

Vicente, Luis Miguel. 1988. "El lamento de Pleberio: contraste y parecido con dos lamentos en *Cárcel de amor*." *Celestinesca* 12 (1): 35–43.

Villalobos, Francisco López de. 1950. *Anfitrión, comedia de Plauto*. Madrid: Atlas BAE 36, 461–93.

Villegas Selvago, Alonso de. 1873. *La comedia llamada Selvagia*. Madrid: Colección de libros raros o curiosos, vol. 5.

Wack, Mary Frances. 1990. *Lovesickness in the Middle Ages*. Philadelphia: University of Pennsylvania Press.

Wardropper, Bruce W. 1964. "Pleberio's Lament for Melibea and the Medieval Elegiac Tradition." *MLN* 79:140–52.

———. 1987. "An Apology for Philology." *MLN* 102:176–90.

Westra, Laura. 1986. "Love and Beauty in Ficino and Plotius." In *Ficino and Renaissance Neoplatonism*, edited by Konrad Eisenbichler and Olga Zorzi Pugliese, 175–87. Toronto: Dovehouse.
Whinnom, Keith. 1966. "The Relationship of the Early Editions of the *Celestina*." *Zeitschrift für Romanische Philologie* 82:22–40.
———. 1977. "El *plebérico corazón* and the authorship of Act I of *Celestina*." *Hispanic Review* 45:195–99.
———. 1980. "The Problem of the 'Best-Seller' in Spanish Golden-Age Literature." *Bulletin of Hispanic Studies* 57:189–98.
Wolters, Al. 1986. "Ficino and Plotius' Treatise 'On Eros.'" In *Ficino and Renaissance Neoplatonism*, edited by Konrad Eisenbichler and Olga Zorzi Pugliese, 189–97. Toronto: Dovehouse.

Index

Abélard, 6, 13
Abulcasim, 58
Agamben, Giorgio, 3 n. 2, 30 n. 61, 63 n. 2, 105
Amadís de Gaula, 65
Amorosa visione, 21–22
Andreas Capellanus, 10, 13, 25, 56, 81
Anfitrión, 6, 27–28
Arcipreste de Talavera, 105
Aristotle, 6, 31–34, 40, 41, 44, 45, 64, 72, 73, 76, 104
Armas, Frederick A. de, 63, 63 n. 2
Asensio, Manuel, 2, 5
Augustine, 37–40, 41, 44, 46
Averroes, 40
Avicenna, 40–41, 42, 44, 46, 58, 72, 73, 76, 101, 101 n. 7

Babb, Lawrence, 12 n. 3, 57 n. 8
Bataillon, Marcel, 3, 71 n. 7, 80, 93, 93 n. 1
Beauvais, Vincent of, 45
Boccaccio, 6, 20–22
Bright, Timothy, 102–3
Burton, Robert, 7, 10–13, 56–57, 63–77, 79, 102, 103, 105–6

Calcidius, 35, 36, 37, 41, 45
Campagnola, Giulio, 107
Cantarino, Vicente, 93 n. 1
Canterbury Tales, 57–58
Cárdenas, Anthony J., 63 nn. 1–2

Carlos V, 27, 75 n. 10
Castells, Ricardo, 3 n. 2, 63, 80 n. 1, 94 n. 2
Castiglione, Baldassare, 7, 57 n. 8, 79–92
Catullus, 64
Cejador y Frauca, Julio, 54–55
Celestina de Palacio, 4, 4 n. 3, 48, 50 n. 4, 94
Cerezo, Mateo, 107 n. 9
Cervantes, Miguel de, 100
Chaucer, Geoffrey, 65
Ciavolella, Massimo, 42 n. 8
Cligés, 6, 14–15
Clitophon and Leucippe, 12
Comedia Selvagia, 5, 6
Comedia Serafina, 4, 6
Comedia Thebaida, 4
Comedia Ypólita, 4
Constantine the African, 56, 58, 63 n. 2
Couliano, Ioan P., 44–45, 57, 86 n. 5, 90 n. 8, 104
Criado del Val, Manuel, 55

Dante, 6, 16–18, 25, 59, 60, 81, 90
De Amore, 10, 81
De Guillaume au faucon, 15–16
Deyermond, Alan, 4 n. 3, 48 n. 2, 71 n. 7, 80, 81, 97 n. 4, 108 n. 11, 109 n. 12, 109–10, 111
Dolce stil nuovo, 14

Don Quixote, 65
Dulaey, Martine, 30 n. 1
Dunn, Peter, 81, 90, 92, 108 n. 11, 109 n. 12
Dürer, Albrecht, 107

Erotomania, 11

Faulhaber, Charles B., 4, 48, 50 n. 4, 94
Fernández, Sebastián, 4
Fernando el Católico, 27, 75 n. 10
Ferrand, Jacques, 11, 59
Ficino, Marsilio, 20 n. 6, 42–43, 42 n. 8, 43 n. 9, 46, 57 n. 8, 72, 73, 76, 85 n. 4, 86 n. 6, 89 n. 7, 90 n. 8, 104
Fin amor, 14
Foreest, Peter van, 59
Fortuna, Bona, 56
Fox, Ruth A., 67
Fraker, Charles F., 24 n. 7, 94 n. 2, 108 n. 11, 110, 112 n. 13

García, Michel, 4 n. 3, 48
García Ballester, Luis, 56 n. 7
Garci-Gómez, Miguel, 4, 9–10, 27 n. 9, 54 n. 5, 55, 55 n. 6, 61, 80 n. 1
Gerard of Berry, 56, 58, 101
Gerli, E. Michael, 108 n. 11
Gilman, Stephen, 3, 5, 93, 93 n. 1, 108–10
Gómez de Toledo, Gaspar, 4
Gómez-Miedes, Bernardino, 65, 75 n. 10
Gordonius, Bernardus, 11 n. 2, 57, 64–65, 71 n. 6
Green, Otis H., 63, 98 n. 5

Harrison, Robert Pogue, 14
Héloïse, 6, 13, 25
Heraclitus, 97, 107
Hildegard of Bingen, 41–42, 46
Hippocrates, 24 n. 7

Isabel, Queen, 75 n. 10

Jackson, Stanley W., 12 n. 3

Jacquart, Danielle, 56 n. 7
Juana la Loca, 75 n. 10

Kassier, Theodore L., 67 n. 4
Klibansky, Raymond, 24 n. 7, 56 n. 7, 106, 107 n. 10
Kristeller, P. O., 42 n. 8
Kruger, Steven F., 30 n. 1, 34, 39 n. 6

L'elegia di Madonna Fiammetta, 6, 20–21
La Dorotea, 5
La vita nuova, 6, 16–18, 59, 81
Lacarra, María Eugenia, 71 n. 7, 80, 81
Laurentius, Andreas, 56 n. 7
Lida de Malkiel, María Rosa, 3, 10, 54, 60, 67, 81, 92, 93, 93 n. 1, 100, 108 n. 11
Lilio de Medicina, 11 n. 2, 57, 64–65, 71 n. 6
López de Villalobos, Francisco, 6, 27 n. 10, 27–28
Lowes, John Livingston, 12 n. 3, 57–58

Macrobius, 35, 37, 40, 45
Madrigal del Tostado, Alfonso, 12 n. 2
Maravall, José Antonio, 71 n. 7, 80
Marciales, Miguel, 49 n. 3, 51, 54
Martial, 53, 55
Martin, June Hall, 56, 63, 71 n. 7, 80, 81
Martorell, Joanot, 60
Maurer, Christopher, 25 n. 8
McGrady, Donald, 4 n. 3, 48, 55 n. 6, 62 n. 10
McVaugh, Michael R., 56 n. 7
Medici, Cosimo de', 42 n. 8
Medici, Lorenzo de', 22–25, 85 n. 4, 90 n. 9
Menéndez Pelayo, Marcelino, 10
Menéndez Pidal, Ramón, 52, 53, 54, 54 n. 5
Michael, Ian, 4 n. 3, 48, 48 nn. 1 and 2
Michelangelo, 107
Moffit, John F., 107

Oribasius, 58, 72, 73

Palley, Julian, 25 n. 8
Panofsky, Erwin, 24 n. 7, 56 n. 7, 106, 107 n. 10
Parker, A. A., 3
Paulus, 10
Pereda, Antonio, 107 n. 9
Petrarca, 6, 18–19, 64, 97, 111
Pineda, Juan de, 99–100, 101
Plato, 6, 30 n. 2, 30–31, 45, 57 n. 8, 83
Plutarch, 72, 73
Proaza, Alonso de, 48, 96–97
Puebla de Montalván, 103

Rhazes, 40
Ribera, José de, 107, 107 n. 9
Rico, Francisco, 48 n. 2
Rime in morte di Madonna Laura, 6, 18–19, 19 n. 5
Riquer, Martín de, 2, 3, 52–53, 54 n. 5
Rubens, Peter Paul, 107
Ruggerio, M. J., 101 n. 7
Rumeau, Aristide, 3
Russell, P. E., 51–52, 54, 62 n. 10

Santa Croce, Girolamo da, 107
Saxl, Fritz, 24 n. 7, 56 n. 7, 106, 107 n. 10
Segunda Celestina, 4, 6
Sem Tob, Rabbi, 25 n. 8
Seneca, 64, 66
Sennert, Daniel, 56, 59

Severin, Dorothy S., 1 n. 1, 3, 12 n. 2, 48 n. 2, 50, 54, 71 n. 7, 80, 81, 98 n. 5, 108 n. 11
Shipley, George, 80 n. 1, 108 n. 11
Silva, Feliciano de, 4
Snow, Joseph, 108 n. 11
Solomon, Michael, 55 n. 6, 63, 63 nn. 1 and 2
Soufas, Teresa S., 60 n. 9
Stamm, James R., 3, 71 n. 7, 80
Synesius of Cyrene, 34

Tatius, Achilles, 12
Tercera Celestina, 4, 6
Tirant lo Blanc, 60
Tragedia Policiana, 4, 6
Trotter, G. D., 55
Troyes, Chrétien de, 6, 14–15
Truesdell, W. D., 3

Vega, Lope de, 5
Vicente, Luis Miguel, 108 n. 11
Vilanova, Arnaldus de, 59
Villegas Selvago, Alonso, 4–5, 6
Vives, Luis, 65, 100

Wack, Mary Frances, 12 n. 3, 24 n. 7, 42 n. 7, 56, 56 n. 7, 101
Wardropper, Bruce W., 49–50, 61, 94 n. 3, 108 n. 11
Westra, Laura, 42 n. 8
Whinnom, Keith, 53–54, 94 n. 2, 114
Wolters, Al, 42 n. 8

www.ingramcontent.com/pod-product-compliance
Lightning Source LLC
Chambersburg PA
CBHW031554300426
44111CB00006BA/305